Almost Full Circle

Almost Full Circle

A Tribute to Dad

Steven Michael Hubele

Copyright © 2010 by Steven Michael Hubele.

Library of Congress Control Number: 2009912880
ISBN: Hardcover   978-1-4500-0893-8
               Softcover   978-1-4500-0892-1

All rights reserved. No part of this book may be reproduced or transmitted in any form or by any means, electronic or mechanical, including photocopying, recording, or by any information storage and retrieval system, without permission in writing from the copyright owner.

This book was printed in the United States of America.

To order additional copies of this book, contact:
Xlibris Corporation
1-888-795-4274
www.Xlibris.com
Orders@Xlibris.com
69723

CONTENTS

ACKNOWLEDGMENTS 7

PREFACE 9

INTRODUCTION 13

DOWN THE FINAL STRETCH 17

THE EARLY YEARS 25

"TALK ABOUT A DEFINING MOMENT IN ONE'S LIFE" 37

"FATHERHOOD" 44

"GOLF AND FISHING" 72

"PAPER BOY" 87

"DANCING WITH BEES" 101

"BAD MEALS" 122

"TRIPS TO ALASKA AND HAWAII" 133

"EDUCATION" 152

"DANGEROUS WATERS" 166

"CARDINALS BASEBALL" 170

"FAREWELL" 189

FOOTNOTES AND ILLUSTRATION CREDITS 197

INDEX 199

ACKNOWLEDGMENTS

During my life, I have received much help along the way. My childhood was a curiously good one, thanks to my parents, George and Audrey Hubele. This book is mostly an earthy recounting of growing up in St. Louis during the 1950s and 1960s, overcoming some tragic events and Midwest life for decades way beyond that. As the years were passing by, change was happening faster than we took the time to notice.

Everything written in this book happened and is true, with a slight bit of embellishment just for fun. My family knew how to have fun.

I would like to thank my sisters, Kathy, Karen, and Patricia, for the abundance of material and experiences we shared during our formative years. Thank you to my daughters, Amanda and Allison, for the experiences during their formative years.

I remain especially grateful to my publisher for significantly broadening the availability of *Almost Full Circle,* helping to expand its presence from word-of-mouth sales to the online market and brick-and-mortar bookstores. Also, many thanks to the staff at St. Louis County Library and all my teachers through the years at Dressel Kindergarten, St. Simons Elementary, St. John Vianney High School,

St. Louis Community College at Meramec, Southeast Missouri State University, and graduate school professors at Webster University.

Thanks to my father, George Walter Hubele, for all the years of a wonderful relationship we had before his death in 2004. Rest in peace.

Thanks to my mother, Audrey Margaret Hubele, for her tremendous courage and all she continues to do for her children and grandchildren, ever since recovering from quintuplet bypass and heart-valve replacement surgery in 2008.

If any readers spot mistakes in this book, please feel free to e-mail me a letter. The mistakes were unintentional.

PREFACE

Ten years have passed since I started writing the manuscript of *Almost Full Circle*. Writing a book or screenplay is a huge undertaking and a time-consuming project. One must make a commitment not normally needed in everyday life. To write successfully, you have to be alone in a quiet room, with day-to-day chores completed and plenty of available free time on hand to think, with conscious picking and choosing of words to develop and tell your story.

The Bible is the best-selling single-volume book of all time, printed in any language, nearing an estimated seven billion copies. While some claim divine inspiration, other scholars and people of different faith traditions do not accept supernatural authorship, while everyone recognizes centuries of enormous amounts of time and devotion to this great series of works. According to my research, Johannes Gutenberg's first major work was the printing of the Bible on one of the first movable-type presses in the year 1455.

The list of the three all-time best-selling book series includes Perry Rhodan, Star Wars, and Harry Potter. Perry Rhodan, written in over two thousand versions, penned in German, and first published in 1961 by various authors, sold approximately one billion copies. Star Wars, written in two hundred installments and first published in 1977 by various authors, sold approximately 750 million copies. Harry Potter was first published in 1997 by J. K. Rowling after numerous rejections from other publishers; the earliest six installments sold approximately 500 million copies.

Publisher's Weekly estimates that over one billion copies of Agatha Christie's novels sold in English and another billion sold in other languages.

The Poky Little Puppy, authored by Janette Sebring Lowrey in 1942, and *Charlotte's Web*, authored by E. B. White in 1952, are two of the all-time best-selling children's books.

Twenty-first century publishers monitor the performances of self-published books in a sort of Darwinian selection process and see what works rise to the top, like tryouts for the baseball team. Since the onset of YouTube, Facebook, and MySpace, self-publishing is not whimsical anymore.

Just naming the title of a book can be a daunting task. *A Funny but Serious Story*; *Read This, It Might Be a Hit*; *The World According To Steve*; *Burdens of Life*; and *Just for Laughs* are just a few titles I kicked around for my book. I decided on *Almost Full Circle* to be the title in hopes that the reader would want to know more. This book is a piece of work, written from the trenches of my life in honor of my father and mother.

If this story converts into a box-office hit movie, I would like Ron Howard to travel to St. Louis, Missouri, to be the director of the movie. In 2007, state legislators enacted a law that provides a tax break for investors in Missouri-made movies. This author and Ron Howard were born one week apart in March of 1954. Ron is an admired actor, but his work as a director in films and his loyalty to his close-knit family are what seem to make him a happy man. He filmed the movie *Cocoon* in the Bahamas, so a visit to some remote exotic place is another possibility. Went this far already, what the heck; Brad Pitt, another boy who grew up in Missouri, can play me. If for some reason director Ron Howard and actor Brad Pitt do not get along, I may have blown any opportunities on the first pages of this book. Oh well, risk is part of life and we have to take chances to reap rewards.

INTRODUCTION

My book is dedicated to my parents, George and Audrey Hubele, who helped me through the good times and the bad times growing as a human being living in the Midwest. From my parents, I learned my storytelling skills. The biggest gift they gave to their children was to tell us bedtime stories of the olden days. Dad's stories usually involved street smarts, exciting stuff like undercover work by spies, submarines blowing up enemy ships, or play-by-play game enactments of past champions with gestures and sound effects. Dad listened when a kid told him a story, too. He made you feel your stories were important.

Mom's stories usually involved something interesting she read or something she saw on television. Her stories usually involved lessons about good morals or topics she thought good mothers tell their children. She made sure her children did their chores and homework, and because of this, her children knew she cared about them.

Most important, I must thank Harry Dick. Had he not taken the risk of mentoring me during this book-writing process, none of this would be happening. Harry's contributions are evident throughout the chapters in this book. I would be remiss if I failed to say a simple "thank you" to him for his vision and patience. Seriously, Harry had nothing to do with the inception of this book, but my father (George) did once sell a life insurance policy to a man named Harry Dick. Sad, but true, that really was his name. What kind of parents would attach such a name to a baby?

Most people have a few defining moments in their lives. Classic stuff such as birth; graduation from high school or college; marriage, career; and our assortment of family, friends, and acquaintances have a huge effect on our lives. We ask ourselves, "Who loves me? Where should I work, where is my next paycheck coming from? Do we drive a decent car? Do we have a great view from our condominium or a safe home in a good neighborhood? Are we making a difference in this world?" Our lives are unique works of art.

We all have that fire burning inside, but sometimes it just goes away because we never get the opportunity to use it. Sometimes, our spirit is broken, and there does not seem to be any hope for progress. Why do I not get any of the breaks? What is the truth? We could spend a lot of time on debates or discussions central to the development of this concept. However, if we work hard, overcome obstacles, and are honest with ourselves and other people, we will have more opportunities to feel good about our choices. I have learned that the only way you are going to get anywhere in life is by working hard. Whether you are a doctor, writer, athlete, construction worker, or businessperson, there is no substitution for it. If you work hard, you win. If you do not, you will not. Nevertheless, try to have a little fun along the way.

In this book, I will try to tell you about some of the defining moments relating to my life and work experiences. Some of my life experiences were difficult or complicated, while others were routine or simple, but I usually tried to find the humor in things in order to overcome the burdens of life, coming to terms with jobs, marriage, raising children, friendships, and the loss of a loved one. Sometimes, life feels like more of a burden than a benefit. However, it is important to maintain wit and perspective in spite of hardships or losses while continuing to laugh.

This book does not avoid some tough issues. The chapters are somewhat independent of each other, so if one chapter sounds more intriguing, it is all right to skip around from chapter to chapter. However, it is my contention that ultimately, you will want to read all of the chapters because they are entertainingly interesting. Most of the stories have a little humor in them and some have a strange twist to them. Hope you enjoy reading this book, because I loved every minute I spent thinking about it, researching it, and writing it.

DOWN THE FINAL STRETCH

As a young man of seventeen years, George Walter Hubele enlisted in the United States Navy in 1947. He did his basic training at Pearl Harbor in Hawaii and, for the next four years, was delegated to work on submarines as a seaman; part of that time, he was bringing supplies to ships during the Korean War. About that same time, a young woman named Audrey handled clerical chores for the St. Louis archbishop and nursing duties for Dr. Reuter, a general practitioner who had an office in the neighborhood where she lived on St. Louis Avenue.

Upon returning to St. Louis, Missouri, after completing his four-year stint in the Navy, George met an attractive young woman named Audrey Margaret Juengst. George of German decent, who grew up on the south side of St. Louis, and Audrey of Irish decent, who was from the north side of St. Louis, were conservative people and were married on April 18, 1953.

As a young married man, George was a sales manager for a large national insurance firm, offering products from a diverse portfolio, but mainly he concentrated on selling life insurance, health plans, and retirement pensions to individuals and business groups. George was a man with the courage of a Navy seaman, the discretion of a judge, the coordination of an athlete, and the patience of a saint. His naturally curly blonde hair and handsome good looks helped his sales appeal during his early career years of the 1950s. His Pentium-chip brain kept track of things and categorized things as good or bad way before computers existed. People, food, cars, stocks, sports teams all made impressions on him, good and bad.

Four years before getting married, Mom graduated from Laboure High School in 1948, ranked third in a class of eighty-five students, which carried as its reward an offer of a scholarship to St. Louis University, an offer she never accepted, opting to take care of her father. Her father died quite young, long before I was born, due to a long battle with lung cancer, possibly caused by exposure to printing inks and other chemicals at his work site.

Audrey kept her short brown hair combed back and wore little makeup, and her complexion had a soft, healthy glow to it. Audrey's early part of her marriage to George was mostly spent as child-bearing years, raising four children: Steven (me, the oldest), Kathy (the oldest girl), Karen (middle child), and Patricia (the baby). Audrey (Mom) spent most of her time cooking meals, doing laundry, cleaning house, breaking up arguments, and trying to set aside some time to read books. Mom loved to read books, all kinds of books. She held our family together by being kind, sincere, and loving. She was entirely without suspicion, did not spread rumors, and never said a bad word about another person.

Because Dad had a strong Midwest work ethic, working from sunup to sundown, my sisters and I were better off than most people of our socioeconomic background were. Our house was a cozy place with food in the refrigerator, plenty of books and magazines to read, notes with a daily list of each child's chores, and a modest amount of clothes to toss around the two shared bedrooms.

The entire subdivision sat parallel to Kohler's truck farm, an example of a family business that still existed, working the fields in the Heartland of America. Mr. and Mrs. Kohler and their eighty-year-old mother worked the fields of the ten-acre truck farm, wearing large straw hats to protect their faces from the sun as they picked mostly tomatoes and strawberries. Atop the hill next to the farm, our house was the first address on Lawnbrook Drive, east of Baptist Church Road on the south side of St. Louis County. The Pevely Dairy milkman delivered milk (usually two gallons of 2 percent), processed at the Grand Avenue city location, to our front porch on Mondays and Thursdays.

Our house was a ranch-style house with a coarse gray-shingled siding, asphalt roof, and green shutters built on a larger lot than most, with the biggest backyard in the subdivision. The backyard doubled as the neighborhood athletic field; we played football and soccer during the winter, while we played baseball and softball in the summer. Games ended when Mom decided it was time for all kids to go home to eat dinner. The only downside to Mom's cooking was the smell of the kitchen on the nights we had to eat "rush and puff" for dinner. This recipe has been in my Mom's family since my grandmother got it from her mother. Rush and puff (my sisters and I called it ruff and tough . . . we would rather eat fruitcake), served about once per week, was Mom's version of a noodle casserole, a mixture of fresh or canned green peas, fresh broccoli, long stringy flat lasagna noodles, and a special cheese sauce without the sesame seed bun.

"Just eat a little bit and leave what you do not like," Mom would say.

"We don't like any of it, Mom," my sisters and I would say in perfect unison.

Sprinkling on lots of salt and pepper, pinching your nose closed, and rushing to eat this stuff did not make it taste better, but feeding it to the dog or unsuccessfully attempting to wrap it up and smoke it, did ease our pain.

Dad brought our dog, a purebred beagle, home from work one hot summer day as a surprise. Her name was Bitsy; this was a combination of Mom's preferred choice of naming her Little Bits (she was a tiny toy beagle) and Dad's choice of naming her Shitsie (she pooped a lot). The beagle became the most popular purebred dog in 1954 America, according to the American Kennel Club. The cocker spaniel ruled for the seventeen previous years. Approximately fifty thousand purebred beagles roamed America and another twenty million mutts (some barked louder and pooped more than the purebreds) claimed part-beagle status. In the Midwest, if you feed your dog, give it water, and take your dog for an occasional walk, you treated your dog well. In Beverly Hills, Ca, where things are sometimes weirdly different, people pay one hundred dollars an hour for a massage for their dogs.

The year of Steven's (author of this book) birth, 1954, was the fulcrum of America in the twentieth century, when the United States balanced between World War II on one side and the Vietnam War on the other. At the time, people were just trying to make things work, spending time with their families, going to church, being involved with their communities, and trying to have a little fun and survive the summer heat. On July 14, 1954, thermostats reached a scorching 115 degrees, as hot as it has ever been in St. Louis in over one hundred years of keeping weather records.

Most households shared one car. The hot car everybody talked about in 1954, the Thunderbird manufactured by Ford, became the company's first production sports car sold on the open market. It boasted a V-8 engine, with a four-barreled carburetor that topped out at 160 horsepower. The Thunderbird's sticker price started at three thousand dollars. During the late 50s, the American car buyer had more than three hundred models to choose from at new car dealerships. Ford, General Motors, American Motors, and Chrysler had no second thoughts of worrying about competition from Japan, Germany, or any other country in the world. Pilots of the first commercial jet, the Boeing 707, built for transcontinental travel and capable of carrying over two hundred passengers and flying at six hundred miles per hour, started overseas flights in 1954.

People did not worry about or even contemplate terrorism, swine flu, airport security, cyberspace security, nuclear threats, immigration border control, or many of the other functions of homeland security. However, antiwar demonstrations, civil rights conflicts, political assassinations, and the drug culture of the late 60s were right around the corner and would become almost daily topics of the evening news. With the assassinations of John F. Kennedy, Robert Kennedy, and Martin Luther King, some of the people of our nation lost some of their hopes and dreams of the potential for things getting better.

My family had most of the things we needed, but we also learned to share and make sacrifices. As a young boy, just hanging out with Dad was especially fun for me, just Dad and me. Dad liked to drive to work on Saturdays to check his mail and do paperwork at his office on West Florissant Avenue. Sometimes, I would get to ride along. I would give anything at all to ride to work with Dad just once more on a Saturday morning. A stroll around the office with Dad usually became a satisfying experience—interesting because you got the chance to eat free donuts or meet men like Johnny Roland or Willis Crenshaw, NFL football players, all-star running backs for the St. Louis Cardinals who made public appearances and actually worked at the office during the off-season. Mr. Crenshaw wore size 16 wide shoes; big feet are a favorable advantage for NFL running backs trying to keep their balance while attempting to run over middle linebackers and stomping on defensive coverage two secondary players.

Sometimes we would stop at Woolworth's on the way home to look at coins (we collected wheat pennies and buffalo nickels as a hobby), buy a goldfish or fish food, or just sit at the lunch counter inside the store for good conversation and a good meal. Once, my sister Kathy put the store-bought fish food in her underwear drawer for safekeeping and forgot about it. The fish food, left undisturbed for several days because we must have been feeding the fish with table scraps, attracted water bugs galore to the bedroom that all four of us kids shared. Upon discovering this misfortune, Dad flushed Goldie (my fish) and Blackie (my sister Kathy's fish) down the toilet. Goldie and Blackie were two two-year-old goldfish, considered old by many for fish living in a fishbowl. Perhaps Goldie and Blackie lived the rest of their lives with much more freedom, swimming in Gravois Creek, the runoff stream where they ended up after the flush on that fateful day.

On one bright sunny Saturday in July of 1961, it was just Dad and I and we decided to do something different. Dad and I went to Fairmont Park Racetrack in Fairmont City, Illinois to bet on the thoroughbred horses. I was only seven years old and certainly could not bet, but I could watch those beautiful creatures run. Fairmont Park is a grade III racing track and an official waging parlor of the Illinois State Racing Commission. At the ripe old age of seven, this was my first time to go to a thoroughbred-racing track, a very memorable experience for sure.

If you trace your ancestry back twenty generations, you would find that you have over a million grandparents, making one believe that all of us somehow are related. My great-great-grandfather, George Hubele, was born on December 11, 1806, in Wuettenberg, Germany. He and his younger brother, Carl, a thirty-seven-year-old cultivator and horse trainer, arrived in New York at Ellis Island in 1850. According to records from the Historical Research Center, the brothers sailed to New York onboard a ship called the "Cotton Planter." Bearers of the Hubele or Hubel surname were granted "The Lamb of Arms," which was a family document symbolizing the planet Mars and military fortitude and honor. It symbolizes the moon and denotes constancy, persistence, hard work, obedience, and peace. My great-grandfather's name was George, and so was my grandfather's, accordingly. I was never able to meet my grandfather (Dad's father), George Hubele, because he died in 1947, seven years before I was born. These aforementioned bits of information about our family history tell the reader a little more about us.

Upon entering the freshly painted front gates at Fairmont Racetrack in Fairmont City, Illinois, approximately ten miles east of the downtown area of St. Louis, Missouri, Dad paid for our admission tickets, a one-dollar racing program, and a yellow tip sheet. The first race was about to start in ten minutes. I remember being awestruck by the huge tote board and all the fancy glowing lights. I was impressed by the 1960s technology, in that all the numbers and dollar amounts seemed to change at such a rapid pace. "How were the betting parlor clerks able to keep the odds current and up to the minute?" I thought.

After we pondered over all the entries for the first race, Dad noticed that the number ten horse bore the name "Grandpa's Horse." Grandpa's Horse was a long shot bet at 99 to 1 odds. For sentimental reasons, Dad and I decided that each of us would wager two dollars to win on Grandpa's Horse.

After hearing the starting gun sound, we looked over and saw that all of the horses got out of the starting gate in somewhat good fashion. Within a few seconds and with much newly found anticipation, we heard the track announcer say, "Grandpa's Horse, a frontrunner, has taken the early lead." We watched the rest of the horses on the far side of the racetrack, and in an instant, the number ten flashed next to the "*WIN*" position on the large electronic tote board. It was too early to jump up and down with joy, but the excitement of getting your horse's number called was a lot of fun. As the rest of the bunched group of horses rounded the first turn, we heard the announcer say, "Grandpa's Horse has increased his commanding lead by three lengths." Dad looked at me with a wink and a reserved smile, as if to signal that he knew something that I did not, but 99 to 1 shots very seldom win races, so I tried not to become too optimistic. Shortly thereafter, all the horses seemed to vanish from my sight. Mainly, this was due to all of the taller adults, who were increasingly congregating in front of us in anticipation of a great finish to the race.

For a few brief moments, as time seemed to stand still, my heart started to race and I wondered what was happening. All of the sudden, the track announcer (speaking in a much firmer and louder voice) shouted, "Around the final turn they go, it's Grandpa's Horse by ten lengths; no other horse is going to catch him now." By this time, the crowd was uneasy and Dad and I were jumping up and down with joy. I was starting to think about how each of us could spend two hundred dollars apiece.

"Down the final stretch, here comes Grandpa's Horse by 15 lengths, a 99 to 1 long-shot," screamed the track's public address announcer. Soon, my dad taking a very satisfying short walk to the payout window to collect our winnings would be imminent.

As Grandpa's Horse approached the finish line, only a mere quarter-furlong away from the finish wire, our fate took a dramatic twist. As if to be struck down by a flash of lightning, Grandpa's Horse stumbled and then fell to the ground. Just a few strides short of reaching the finish line, he suffered a massive fatal heart attack. We watched, as all of the other horses would pass ahead at the finish. Grandpa's Horse, the fastest horse, trying to run with all of his heart, lay alone motionless in the middle of the racetrack. Stunned and saddened, everyone watched, as the groundskeepers hauled away our dead horse on a square wooden skid pulled by a large John Deere tractor. Our thrilling anticipation turned to total disbelief, and there was nothing we could do to change our empty feelings. When I get to heaven, maybe, just maybe, Grandpa will be able to explain it all to me.

The memories remain.

THE EARLY YEARS

The landmarks of my childhood consisted of Dressel School, St. Simon Church and School, Concord Bowling Lanes and Pool, Big D's Basement, the Woods, Gravois Creek, Baker's Field, the Confectionary, Heimburger's Bakery, Ronnie's Drive-In, Velvet Freeze, Lou's Sinclair Gas station and Kohler's Farm. All of these places were part of the business district and suburb of South County, something like a small city outside of the big city of St. Louis. South Lindbergh Boulevard runs through it like an old-fashioned main street, storefronts, restaurants, and retail establishments on both sides and houses behind the businesses. Social problems such as terrorism, global warming, the deteriorating environment, and diminishing biodiversity never entered my mind or the mind of any other child in my neighborhood and beyond.

Missouri state law mandated that all five-year-olds must go to kindergarten. Catholic schools near our neighborhood did not offer kindergarten, so all kids within the area school district went to Dressel Public School to meet the requirement. Within the first few days of kindergarten, a serious first crush for Debbie Hilarious resided within my being. About halfway through the school year, as Debbie Hilarious was getting off the bus, she fell on the icy sidewalk as she was running toward the entrance doors to the school. She scraped both of her knees and was crying sitting on the sidewalk. Upon seeing this happen firsthand, immediately my instincts directed me to run to the nurse's station inside the principal's office to get two Band-Aids for my crush. The nurse returned with me to apply the Band-Aids and console my crush, Debbie Hilarious. One week later, Debbie Hilarious hit me over the head with her lunchbox. No clear reason ever given suggested why she did this to me. My crush, pardon the pun, ended at that moment.

On Saturday nights in the early sixties, my parents would drop off my buddies and me at the Granada Show, one of several great movie theatres in St. Louis, which are since long gone. For thirty-five cents, you were able to buy one admission ticket and for another thirty-five cents, you were able to purchase a large plastic cup full of Coca-Cola from the large stainless steel soda fountain, a box of Dots (multicolored fruit-flavored licorice drops), and a generously large box of salted buttered (real butter) popcorn. All this was very satisfying to kids under fifteen with healthy digestive tracts.

The longest running movie ever at the Granada Show, *The One-Eyed Monster*, played all summer one year. This movie scared the crap out of any kid under ten years of age and even some much older. Sometimes the spoken words you heard did not match the movement of the Japanese actors' lips. The music appeared to get louder at the wrong times, but this did not matter. *The One-Eyed Monster* was darn scary. My friends Toad, Tad (Toad's younger brother), Big D, Mark Bigley, Hoosie, and Becker probably saw the movie at least ten times. I went another five times with my dad.

One-Eyed beat the heck out of the original sissy movie, *Winnie the Pooh*, which I was forced to see with my sisters and again with my friends at some kid's birthday party that started with all of us meeting at the Granada Show.

A person and how many trips that person took to the bathroom judged good movies. If the movie was a great movie, a person sat in the theatre and just let the bladder fill up to capacity and beyond, no trips to the bathroom. If a movie stunk, a person may make two trips to the bathroom, three trips to the concession stand, and maybe a trip outside to look for loose change in the cracks of the sidewalk in front of the theatre. Looking for change was chancy because you might not get back in the theatre, unless you had a friend who could sneak you back in the side door, when the manager with the flashlight was not looking.

In 1960, St. Simons Church opened its doors to my family and the rest of the congregation. The church was brand-new and part of the building doubled as seating for the elementary school cafeteria during the week when classes were in session. I recall one particularly rushed Sunday morning getting ready for mass at St. Simons Church. I put on the same pair of brown uniform pants that I wore to school on the previous Thursday and Friday. The brown pants needed to be washed, but hell (I mean heck . . . better talk for a Catholic boy going to church), this saved time, we were in a hurry, and my family needed to get to church on time. I was twelve years old and going through my first growth spurt.

We made it to mass on time and my family shared a pew with another family near the back of the church. We usually sat in the row according to height: Dad, Mom, Steve, Kathy, Karen, Patti. Patti (the baby) always wandered back toward Mom early on during the proceedings and sat next to her. For some reason, the mass was shorter, much shorter than most other Sunday masses. Even the sermon was much shorter than usual. Perhaps our parish priest, Father Dierker, was not feeling well this day.

When mass was over, my family walked back to the car, a white 1959 Ford Fairlane station wagon, together. Soon after we all took our seats and slammed all the car doors closed (you had to slam the big heavy steel car doors back then in order to get them closed), my dad blurted out, "Steve, you need to buy some new pants, your balls are hanging out," instead of saying, "Steve, your pants are too tight and high-water short,"

Dad had his own way of driving across his cause of contention, direct to the point. Right in front of my mom and my sisters, Dad was telling me this. Perhaps he thought my sisters were too young to understand what he was talking about at the time. This taught me that dads could not be afraid to tell their children things or help them at any time, even if their words totally embarrass them, make them hyperventilate, or cause them to run away from home. Maybe he wanted me to get a job and pay for my own pants.

I wondered if any of the girls in my sixth grade class in school on Thursday and Friday thought that my balls hung out. Whatever was behind Dad's strategy, it worked. Within a couple of weeks, I had new pants and a job at Concord Bowling Lanes and Swimming Pool. I earned seventy-five cents an hour and worked all summer for three hundred dollars. My wardrobe, though improved, was not great; but I did now own a couple of new pants. Not many minimum wage child-labor laws, if there were any such laws in the fifties or sixties, were enforced. I cut grass, cleaned locker rooms, picked up cans and bottles, collected money from patrons at the front counter, called for emergency help, saved an unsupervised toddler from drowning in the kiddie pool on a slow day, and basically did anything they asked me to do. Working allowed me to buy my own pants for the time being, pants that fit a growing teenager.

From the late thirties through to the early fifties, my great-uncle from Mom's side of the family, John Veldon, managed a restaurant and lounge called Elliot's, adjacent to the old Statler Hotel. The Statler Hotel was built in 1917, just before the start of a period of lavish living during the Roaring Twenties in St. Louis. Local citizens and out-of-towners marveled at the grandeur of the hotel, a hub of activity and a gathering place for high society or anyone who could afford to stay there. The Statler Hotel was the grandest hotel in the city and the first in the country to have air-conditioning unit and a bathroom in every room. From providing paper and ink pens for correspondence to a light in the closet and a chocolate on the pillow, the travel guest enjoyed a high level of luxury. The twenty-story, 650-room hotel featured lavish rooms and an arcaded lobby on the first floor with a fancy ballroom at the top.

Professional ballplayers patronized this establishment because the food was great, the service was great and the restaurant always kept clean. Located near the eastern edge of the wholesale district at Ninth and Washington Avenues, the restaurant was a short distance from the ballpark. After a Cardinals game during the summer of 1958, Dad and I paid a visit to eat dinner and say hello to Uncle John at Elliot's. During the visit, Uncle John presented me with an autographed baseball signed by the entire '44 World Champion Cardinals team. The ball became a cherished memento displayed on a bookshelf in my downstairs bedroom.

In the fifties, many families remodeled their basements, adding a bedroom or two to make extra living space for their growing families. Mr. Pieper, a neighbor and a hobbyist carpenter with eight children, built eight cubicle size rooms in the basement of his house so each child could have their own bedroom.

One hot summer day in 1963, Dad invited a coworker's family, the Simpers, to our house for a barbecue in the backyard. To me, the father was Mr. Simper; the mother was Mrs. Simper, and the son was named Skippy. All members of both our families sat in lawn chairs set up in the backyard, listening to Harry Carey and Jack Buck broadcast the Cardinals game on the radio, except Skippy. Skippy had decided to try to stay cool inside the house, positioning his chair close to a window fan and watching a black-and-white television show, so we thought. When the barbecue pork steaks were done cooking and it was time to go inside the house to eat, both families congregated around the dinner table.

At the dinner table, Skippy suspiciously questioned me saying, "Hope you did not mind me signing the baseball on your bookshelf downstairs?" Immediately, my legs sped my body down to my basement bedroom in front of my bookshelf, like an Olympic sprinter trying to get to the finish line. Nervously picking up the ball off its display mount, it became abundantly clear that Skippy Simper had personalized my '44 Cards team autographed baseball with his supersized signature using a black magic marker, completely circling the ball. Though Skippy was two years older and outweighed me by fifty pounds, my inner voice told me to hurt him, hurt him bad. For the sake of Dad's job and for the first time in my life, real self-control stopped any true feelings from springing into action, the evil deed never forgotten. The Simper family never visited our house again.

The following summer of 1964, Dad and I attended a Cardinals game with the Los Angeles Dodgers, with Bob Gibson pitching against Sandy Koufax. We always arrived at the game about one and a half hours early because we enjoyed watching batting practice before the big crowds gathered at the stadium. About thirty minutes into batting practice, Bill White hit a high foul ball about twenty rows back behind the first-base bag. A large, overweight middle-aged man standing about five steps above where the foul ball landed started moving toward the bouncing ball, still rolling in between the rows of seats. Seeing that he might have a chance at getting a ball for his son, Dad, only thirty-three years old and in the prime shape of his life, began leaping over rails like a high jumper on the track team. Upon getting to the ball first, Dad reached down to grab it, firmly placing his hand on top of the ball. The large, overweight middle-aged man, arriving one second late, trying to lay claim to the ball, stepped on Dad's hand, breaking his right thumb. Though his thumb was broken, Dad retrieved the ball for his son.

That same year, on October 4, 1964, the St. Louis Cardinals clinched the National League pennant and later went on to win the World Series. Bill White, all-star first baseman, was a big part of the success of the Cardinals team.

As the St. Louis Cardinals were celebrating their world championship win over the New York Yankees, the St. Simons fourth-grade boys little league team was celebrating their CYC league championship. Several of the coaches organized a team banquet held in the school cafeteria. Mr. Mac and Mr. William, two of our team's great instructional baseball coaches, along with Mr. Bob, an employee of the *St. Louis Post-Dispatch* newspaper, arranged for a special guest speaker at our sports banquet. When the coaches announced the name of the special guest speaker—"Mr. Bill White of the St. Louis Cardinals is here tonight to congratulate and speak to the boys"—my ten-year-old eyes opened wide with excitement. Now I knew why Dad told me to bring the foul ball he retrieved at the Cardinals game earlier that summer to show to my teammates at the banquet.

That night Bill White signed my baseball made me forget about the ruined '44 Cards team autographed baseball, because my dad chased down the ball, handed it over to me, and had it signed by all-star first baseman Bill White. Making the genuine autographed ball even more interesting, years later, a replica of Bill White's signature appeared on all baseballs used during National League games during his reign as president of Major League Baseball.

Conrad Hilton purchased the Statler Hotel in 1954 for $111 million in what was then the world's largest real estate transaction. Hilton sold the hotel in 1968 and it was renamed the Gateway Hotel. The hotel closed down in 1987 after it underwent a mysterious and oft-litigated arson fire the following year. With the need for more hotel space and its prime location across the street from the St. Louis Convention Center, expanded, renovated, and operated by the Marriott Corporation, the hotel reopened in 2004 as the St. Louis Renaissance Grand Hotel. Just as the hotel took on a new name and underwent a new look after renovation, my bookshelf had a new look with a Bill White autographed baseball, replacing a '44 Cardinals team autographed baseball destroyed by a kid named Skippy.

The late fifties was the end of the Big Band Era and easy listening music, but during the early sixties, we entered the music realm of rock and roll. By then, Levi jeans, T-shirts, and Ked's tennis shoes were all boys wanted to wear, and any other kinds of dress pants (with or without balls hanging out) were no longer fashionable or needed. Long hair, tie-dyed shirts, psychedelic colors, love beads, bell-bottom pants, and the peace sign were just a couple years around the corner. New singers and groups became popular with the help of Dick Clark's *American Bandstand*, the closest thing we had at the time to *American Idol*.

My friends and I hung out in the basement of the house owned by Big D's parents almost every Friday night in the mid-sixties. Big D had the coolest train board, an elaborate miniature city with a train setup on several sheets of plywood, in the whole state of Missouri. The miniature city took up half of the basement space. A regulation-size pool table centered the other side of the basement. Friday nights meant finding out about any new additional ensembles to the train city, numerous games of playing eight ball and listening to music. We listened to lots of music.

Big D had the first record player, the first eight-track player, and the first car, a four-door light blue 1965 Mustang, among our tight-knit group of friends. One of our earliest cruising memories in the Mustang includes a trip to Pizza Hut for a late-night meal, but because we did not have enough money to pay our dinner bill, we had to wash dishes at the midnight hour in the back of the kitchen. Back then, pals pooled their money when any one of us needed something, because being a little short of cash just meant you borrowed and then paid back the next time we got together.

In the sixties, most teenage boys learned to work on their own cars. Changing oil, replacing an air filter or battery, fixing a flat tire, topping of fluids, or washing and waxing the car became routine chores in the driveways of suburbia. Listening to music while working on cars helped develop one's musical tastes as well as taste in cars. Being able to rebuild an engine or a carburetor meant you knew a little something about cars. Among our friends, Hoosie was the go-to guy if you needed help fixing your car.

We listened to soundtracks of Frank Sinatra; Chubby Checkers; The Temptations; The Beach Boys; The Beatles; The Rolling Stones; Elvis Presley; The Turtles; Simon & Garfunkel; Led Zeppelin; The Doors; Sly and The Family Stone; Herb Albert and the Tijuana Brass; James Taylor; Mitch Miller; Peter, Paul and Mary; Connie Francis (my dad thought she was hot); and The Righteous Brothers.

Songs such as "California Girls" by the Beach Boys, "Going out of My Head" by the Imperials, "Hound Dog" by Elvis Presley, and "The Twist" by Chubby Checkers played repeatedly by the local radio stations.

Many families of the 1960s experienced what has been termed the "generation gap." Because of John F. Kennedy's assassination, the Vietnam War, segregation, riots, and marches on Washington, the world was spinning out of control and young people were learning not to trust anyone over thirty years old. There was a lot of confusion and mistrust about many issues going in directions not understood by most people. Sex, drugs, and rock and roll took hold of the American culture.

When John Lennon musically imagined the entire world living as one, it is doubtful he dreamed that Woodstock or anything like it would follow his song.

For three days of peace in August of 1969, half a million young people attended the Woodstock music festival at Max Yasgur's farm, a 600-acre farm in the rural town of Bethel, New York. Bethel, in Sullivan County, is forty-three miles southwest of the town of Woodstock, New York, in adjoining Ulster County. During the sometimes rainy and muddy weekend, thirty-two music acts performed outdoors in front of the concertgoers. It is widely regarded as one of the greatest and most pivotal moments in popular music history.

John Fogerty and his band, Creedence Clearwater Revival, signed the first contract, and everyone else followed to get a piece of the action. Joan Baez, Santana, Joe Cocker, Janis Joplin, Roger Daltrey, Country Joe McDonald, Arlo Guthrie, Richie Havens, and Jimi

Hendrix (arguably the best guitar player of all time), performed at Woodstock. Top bands of the era, including Blood, Sweat and Tears; Sha-Na-Na; The Who; Jefferson Airplane; Sly and the Family Stone; Grateful Dead; Crosby, Stills, Nash and Young; and the Paul Butterfield Blues Band rocked for three days of peace in the outdoors at an Upper New York farm.

Joni Mitchell canceled singing at Woodstock to avoid missing a scheduled appearance on the Dick Cavett Show. Bob Dylan pulled out when his son became ill. Jethro Tull did not perform, but his music played over the public address system. The Moody Blues declined an invitation because they were already booked in Paris. Tommy James and the Shondells declined an invitation. Lead singer Tommy James stated later, "We could have kicked ourselves. We were in Hawaii, and my secretary called and said, 'Yeah, listen, there's this pig farmer in upstate New York that wants you to play in his field.' This is how our secretary explained the event to us. So we passed, and we realized what we had missed a couple of days later."[1]

Our group of friends was still a little too young to consider a road trip to party with the hippies at Woodstock, but they did inject some of their values into our mainstream American lives. A kid named Becker was evolving into the music expert among our friends in the neighborhood. He kept up with latest new bands, organized his extensive record collection, amassed an assortment of flashing lights, and began playing the guitar.

The first moon landing happened just one month prior to the Woodstock festival, and these two events had American teenagers in a cosmic state of mind. Boys wore bell-bottom blue jeans and grew long hair and sideburns; girls burned their bras and wore psychedelic flower-patterned dresses. During the same summer, the motorcycle freedom movie *Easy Rider* had a cult following that my friends and I belonged to, watching it over and over at Ronnie's Theatre, our neighborhood drive-in.

Ronnie's had enough space to park a thousand cars and was the largest of any of the St. Louis area drive-ins. A train located on the premises took patrons for rides around the property before the start of the show and during intermissions. The main entrance with the back of the projector screen facing Lindbergh Boulevard was lit up by huge neon letters. The grounds were beautified with all kinds of flowers, trees and shrubs. The landmark known as Ronnie's since 1948, closed in 1983 and the property was bulldozed to the ground making way for the new investors.

Today, much of the old neighborhood is different, a process that evolved over the past fifty years. Heimburger's Bakery is now a National City Bank; Lou's Sinclair Gas Station is now Pioneer Bank, competing for the same customers as National City Bank. Ronnie's Drive-In and all the land it sat on have been redeveloped into a large shopping plaza, which includes a Wehrenberg's indoor movie theatre complex with a dozen living-room-size theaters and a projection screen one-tenth the size of the old outdoor screen.

We used to play in the woods for hours, running around on trails, building tree houses, or building a dam across the creek. Once, a bunch of us built a dam by pulling out rows of plants and piling them high enough, so that we could walk across the slow-flowing creek waters. Unknowingly, the weeds we uprooted turned out to be poison oak plants. Full-body rashes disguised with calamine lotion caused us to itch and suffer for weeks.

Mr. Kohler owned the farm next to the woods. If he liked you, he allowed you to pick a few tomatoes or strawberries to bring home to your mom. If he did not like you or if you caused trouble in the neighborhood, he might shoot you in the ass with buckshot. The Woods and Kohler's Farm now occupy subdivisions, and so does the land once called Baker's Field.

Baker's Field was a sandlot next to a small apple orchard farm owned by an old woman named Mrs. Baker. Though she kept a messy house, she loved and cared for several animals, including a dog, a cat, a baby lamb, a goat, and any stray that needed her help. No one knew if Mrs. Baker had ever been married, and though we seldom saw her, all the kids that played on the sandlot thought she was a nice old woman for giving us permission to play on her property. She allowed us to drink from her faded-green garden hose, and the water tasted like the garden hose, but we did not care because the water was cold. Baseball, fuss ball (same rules as baseball, but a tennis ball is used), field hockey, and football, depending on the season, attracted kids from two miles away to Baker's Field. Toad, one of the older kids and the commissioner at Baker's Field, once banned the oversize bat used by Big D because he hit too many home runs, causing some kids to tire of chasing the ball. If a bat got broken, Toad decided what kind of nails and tape to use to fix it.

We only get one childhood. We only get one chance at life. The world keeps changing whether we want it to or not, and life moves on; we cannot go back. Along the way, we tame the burdens of the beast, continuing on to the next challenge or obstacle.

Certain songs that we listened to have more significance now than we thought they did years ago. "Free Bird," a song by American Southern rock band Lynyrd Skynyrd, has one of the greatest guitar solos of all time. During live performances, the band often played the long song for over fourteen minutes. "Stairway to Heaven," a song by the English rock band Led Zeppelin, composed by guitarist Jimmy Page and vocalist Robert Plant, is the most requested song of all time on radio stations in the United States.

The neighborhood landscape is different and many of the buildings are gone. The music changes, but the memories remain.

"TALK ABOUT A DEFINING MOMENT IN ONE'S LIFE"

Supposedly, newspapers make more money by writing a little about politics but staying away from too much controversy. I carefully considered whether to write about the subject of abortion. Since my own experience had such a profound impact on my life, I decided to keep this section in the book.

"Talk about a defining moment in one's life!" This foregoing experience sure had an effect on my life. If you really think about it—and do not try to hide behind the notion that you are only taking out a bit of protoplasm—abortion is not just minor surgery that means nothing. In fact, abortion has a tremendous effect on everyone involved. What you are doing is terminating a human life. Life must matter; otherwise, nothing else matters—not money, not material things, not land, not anything. For a woman to proceed with an abortion, she is saying, "My life is more important than this life, my time is more important than anyone else's time, my life is much more important at this time." Abortion is terminating a life and it does not matter whether performed at three weeks, four weeks, or six months. According to the laws of our country, it is okay to kill a fetus, but not okay to light up a cigarette in public places, even though second-hand smoke is dangerous.

Adolf Hitler used the rationale of eugenics, a disturbing belief that selective mating, a movement of controlling heredity or who has the opportunity to be born can improve the human race.

Back in late summer of 1977, my girlfriend had an abortion; we had been dating for almost three years. It was supposed to be happy times; we were looking at engagement rings, I had just graduated from Southeast Missouri State University and was about to embark on the start of a long and industrious career with my girl at my side, offering support. Even though we were just starting out, we would be in healthy financial shape, because my girl had already secured a position at a Commerce Bank location in Kirkwood, an older neighborhood community full of Victorian-style two-level homes. I was working at a manufacturing plant. Anyway, that is how I saw it, but she felt differently.

I will never forget the horrible feeling I felt that day at the physician's office inside the medical facility with combining abortion clinic in Kirkwood, Missouri. One of the charms of Kirkwood is that the city has not lost that delightful old-town square feel. However, the abortion clinic was tucked away in an old red brick two-story building, a building many people do not know even exists, on the north side of the historic district, in the space between city hall and the train station. Early in the morning, one weekday in September of 1977, my girlfriend informed me that she missed her last period, even though she had been taking the birth control pill for many months. She asked me to call my work to take the day off, so that I could take her to the doctor for a pregnancy test. At the time, I was working in the machine shop at the manufacturing facility, making conveyor equipment and automated packaging equipment. This job paid the bills until I could find a job related to my teaching or business degrees.

After arriving at the medical "facility/clinic" I waited nervously in the visitors lounge. On the way to see the doctor, we had briefly talked about what would happen if my girlfriend were pregnant. I stated that we would just have to get married a little sooner than expected, but my girlfriend did express concerns about not being ready to have a baby. I was twenty-three years old; she was twenty years old. I guess I figured that things would work out; besides, I thought we loved each other and when life becomes difficult, most people just try to do the right thing.

After waiting approximately fifteen minutes in the visitors lounge, an assistant nurse walked over to advise me that the results had come back positive. She said, "Your girlfriend went ahead with the abortion, but nothing was formed yet, no fingers or toes." This image of "Gumby" entered my mind, and I did not like her choice of words. Immediately, with this angry abyss formed in my stomach, I raced up a flight of steps and down a long corridor to try to find my girlfriend, knowing that within only a matter of the past few minutes, the doctor had already performed the abortion procedure. As soon as I saw her, immediately, my girlfriend of the past three years did not look or feel the same to me. Though it was very difficult to let go, I realized that the girl that I thought I loved, the girl that I had grown to know for three years, had opposing feelings about a very important life-altering issue and my heart felt like it was in my stomach. I knew everything would be different for the rest of my life. Within just a few minutes, without any consultation to me from a doctor or nurse, without any input from me, my voice did not matter. The woman has the last say about her own body; a decision was made and it was final!

Before we left the building, though I objected to my girlfriend having gone ahead with the abortion, I stopped by the billing office to pay for the procedure. Spending for an abortion in violation of my religious beliefs went against every moral fiber in my body. Taking care of the bill, a dreadful compromise to my true convictions, made me feel like I paid to end the life of my own child. Nevertheless, in the whole scheme of things, paying the money was a minor responsibility, a condition to deal with at the time.

I will never forget the ride home in the car. My girlfriend looked very different to me; down deep, I knew my strong, passionate feelings for her would never be the same. During the long ride home (it was only a twenty-minute ride, but seemed like an eternity), she spoke about the experience when asked.

I inquired, "Did the abortionist doctor or his assistants say anything to you during the procedure?"

She said, "They referred to a step number two and a step number one during the process."

Later I would find that step number two was actually the first process, and this included the suctioning of fluids and lower body parts from the embryonic sac, while step number one referred to the head or remaining parts of the fetus being completely removed from the womb. They had secret terminology to shield everyone from the gruesome reality of the whole event. Apparently, by our best estimates, my girlfriend was approximately four to five weeks pregnant, but we were not given any further information from anyone working at the clinic about this stage of development. Remember, this happened in 1977, at a time when authority could refrain or refuse information, and people did not have easy access to the technological computer age as they do today. I later learned that during the third and fourth weeks of pregnancy, the baby's central nervous system forms and the digestive system, face, and mouth begin to take shape and the heart begins to beat.

One of the things that humanizes us is that we value human life, and those who do not are really of a different order of people. There were no grief counselors back then. There was no funeral to attend. That period was a very hard time. Abortion changes everyone in some way. Wounded after an abortion, both women and men suffer physical, emotional, and spiritual pain. Its results include nightmares, difficulty concentrating, anxiety, anger, guilt, low self-esteem, grief, repression, withdrawal, depression, sadness, and difficulty in personal relationships. I have even heard people label the aftermath of abortion, "post-abortion syndrome," or others talking about having episodes of "anniversary mourning," even after thirty years have passed. I imagine that almost anyone, in self-analysis, in revealing their deepest feelings and inner thoughts, will feel sorrow and sometimes still cry about it. The strength that it takes to overcome the aftermath of an abortion is a quality hard-won over inordinate amounts of time.

For the would-be father, though never touched by a surgical instrument, something inside him dies too. Experiencing only the profound mental affects, he has difficulty sorting his feelings.

Abortion has many victims. Most people think of the baby, the mother, or perhaps even the father. Fatherhood breeds fatherhood; without it, responsibility is much harder to teach. Its victims include siblings of the parents or siblings of the baby, living or in the future. It includes grandparents who will never know their grandchild and even the community, because the general public will never benefit from the life that had been intended. It includes even the people who might have encouraged or facilitated the abortion procedure in some way.

That freedom to exercise choice can actually turn into a lifelong feeling of guilt and misery, not a way to escape responsibility or pain, but more a futile attempt to fight, like one of the worst forms of drudgery.

Shrewd politicians talk smoothly about science, reason, and dialogue, expanding access to abortion, wanting to provide federal funding and praising embryonic stem cell research. It is perplexing when politicians, who say they are pro-abortion, focus their energies on all types of fixes (abstinence, better healthcare, sex education and birth—control, fixing teenage pregnancy) while avoiding the truth—whether their underlying belief is that abortion is right or wrong. If abortion advocates garnered the support of all right-minded people with sound principles, none of these solutions would matter.

Many politicians speak as not to offend anyone and to leave the impression that science and scripture coexist in perfect peace and harmony, avoiding the tough issues in order to try to win a popularity contest. That is how to gain the greatest number of votes, by trying to please everyone by saying nothing offensive or specific.

Adoption is an option. There are more people wanting babies than there are babies available in the United States.

Since *Roe v. Wade* on January 22, 1973, statistics provided by the National Right to Life and Human Life International show that there have been over fifty million abortions performed in the United States. That figure is almost half the amount of babies born between 1965 and 1985, an army of high achievers, who pride themselves on being high-tech-savvy and independent. According to the Association of Reproductive Health Professionals, over five hundred thousand women worldwide have died from illegal or legal abortions since the year 2000.

"As we approach the year 2010, the right to life is not a dead issue in some of our state legislatures. The United States Declaration of Independence states, 'All men are created equal.' Amendment Five of the United States Constitution states, 'No person shall be deprived of life without due process of law.' However, one hundred and fifty years ago, the Supreme Court, in a 7-2 decision, declared that Dred Scott was not a person, but slave property. In 1973, in another similar conclusion in *Roe v. Wade*, the Supreme Court declared that a fetus is not a 'person' and thus remains the exclusive property of a woman to keep or dispose of for whatever reason she deems necessary."[2]

Some of the information in the above paragraph has been written about at length by John Stoeffler, a Missouri resident and cofounder of the *Madison Forum*. His featured articles are a synopsis of discussions about public matters dedicated to upholding the principles of our country. Occasionally published, John's articles appear in the *St. Louis Post-Dispatch* newspaper and the South County Journal.

In Missouri, the following restrictions on abortion were in effect as of January 1, 2008: a woman must receive state-directed counseling and then wait twenty-four hours before making a decision about an abortion procedure, and the parent of a minor must consent before she can have an abortion.

"Today, a baby is a baby when it is convenient. It is tissue when the time is not right. A baby is a baby when miscarriage takes place at two or three months. When an abortion takes place at two or three months, a baby now referred to as just a clump of cells. There is a quote etched into the high ceilings of one of our state's capitol buildings. The quote says, 'Whatever is morally wrong is not politically correct.' Abortion is morally wrong. All life is valuable and all life is a gift. We must cherish the gifts given to us."[3]

The death toll of the Civil War made an enormous impact on lives of surviving members of nineteenth-century American families. In a somewhat similar fashion, abortions take a toll on many twenty-first-century American families.

I think of all the military men and women, the bravest of all human beings, fighting wars in Iraq and Afghanistan. How many aborted babies would have become brave soldiers keeping our military strong, firefighters, or police officers helping to protect the local communities in our great country? How many would have studied to become teachers, helping to educate, or doctors, discovering cures and saving lives? Maybe one of them would have grown up to find a cure for muscular dystrophy or cancer.

Abortion is a horrible tragedy. Getting past all the confusion and emotional pain from this experience would prove one of the biggest hurdles to overcome in my life, though the emotions of the past are never truly gone forever.

The memories remain.

"FATHERHOOD"

My dad taught me that when you tell someone you are going to do something, you do it. He was always a man of his word, and I admired that. "When a man lives with God, his voice shall be as sweet as the murmur of the brook and the rustle of the corn." This is a quote from Ralph Waldo Emerson. If the day ever arrives when I can speak to my two daughters during our everyday routines, and all of our voices are sweet and our word is good, then I will know that we have almost arrived at that point. Softball games, basketball games, soccer games, school plays, meals at the kitchen table, walks in the park, vacations, and special times in our children's lives give us the opportunities to relax and spend satisfying time together. When special occurrences happen in a predictable way, they become traditions that touch a child's heart. Feelings fostered by smiles and laughs, they will be a greater gift to our children than any material thing we could buy for them. Sometimes, however, the truly special moment takes everyone by surprise.

At the age of thirty, I became a proud father. My first daughter, Amanda Marie, was born on July 15, 1984, exactly fifteen years later from the day the astronauts landed on the moon; she gleamed of an entirely beautiful and healthy glow. Amanda is an English-Latin-Italian origin name that means lovable, worthy, and intelligent, and it certainly fit her. Seeing her and holding her for the first time changed my life, gave me purpose, made me feel special and proud, so blessed with her as my daughter. My second daughter, Allison Nicole, was born on May 19, 1991; she too was very beautiful and healthy. Allison is an Irish Gaelic-Old German name meaning "truthful and famous among the gods." The name Allison evokes an image of a pretty woman who is graceful, confident, bright, caring, and demure.

The early stages of child-raising years are routine for most mothers, with changing diapers, feedings, naps, and lots of baby talk. At ages two through five, children really begin to get their personality and their fathers redefine their own. Fathers discover a new appreciation for patience and strong absorbent paper towels, working best together, cleaning up spilled milk, orange juice, and the dreaded grape juice accident. Since fathers do not want to be sharks in dirty waters, this home cleanup work makes them feel ready for much bigger cleanups or the possibility of another Valdez Oil Spill.

For me, for better or for worse, fatherhood is most interesting when children start school and most challenging when they become teenagers. Our job as a parent is to teach our children to be independent thinkers and prepare them to be able to take care of themselves. Following are a few of the fun events that I shared with my two daughters, Amanda Marie and Allison Nicole.

On this morning, on a Monday in late August of 1989, Amanda went to school (kindergarten), not counting preschool at daycare, for the first time. That evening, I remember sending her to bed at 9:00 p.m. because her days were longer and more regimented. After tucking her in and leaving her room, this is what transpired between us.

> Amanda: Dad, I need you.
> Dad: What do you want now?

> Amanda: I'm thirsty; can you bring me a drink of water?
> Dad: No, please go to sleep, you have a long day ahead of you!

Ten minutes passed and I assumed that there would be peace and quiet in the house for the rest of the evening, until all of the sudden!

> Amanda: Dad, I need you?
> Dad: What do you want now?
> Amanda: I'm thirsty. Can I have a drink of water?
> Dad: I said *no*! If you ask again, I'll have to give you a spanking!

Approximately ten more minutes passed, but this time I assumed nothing!

> Amanda: Dad, I need you?
> Dad: What do you want now?
> Amanda: When you come in to give me a spanking, could you bring me a drink of water?

Memorable events are so special for parents during the period when their children are young. That is because they wish they could just forget about some of the others. Children try on new thoughts and opinions the way they try on new clothes. They test out opinions on their parents, the same ones they hear at school or from their friends in the neighborhood. Since fathers spend much of their day learning how to do better at their jobs, helping to do the teaching when it involves our children is not supposed to be a problem.

In early spring, 1997, my daughter Amanda, much older now, had her permit and could not wait until she was old enough to get her driver's license. She would have to wait until July 19, 1997, her sixteenth birthday.

Most midterm teenage daughters moan, groan, lash out, and make guttural sounds at attempts by their fathers to talk with them. A lot of the time, because of all the hormones, physiological changes, and brain development, they are impulsive and say things they do not really mean. Whenever my daughters and I were riding in the car together, I realize that I constantly talk about how things used to be and what used to be on that parcel of land before they constructed that building. Looking out the driver's side window of the car, out over South Lindbergh Boulevard in South St. Louis County, seeing the grove of fast-food restaurants, chain convenience store-type gas stations, banks, and car dealerships, I contemplate remembering the open fields where kids played ball and wooded areas that grew trees in their place. Whenever my conversation drifted into moments in the past, Amanda's usual response was, "Dad, you told me that five times already," and she was probably right.

Amanda liked to have free rein and control of the car radio dial. Whenever I would sing, she would say, "Dad, please don't mess up my song, don't sing the words you know, and don't sing the parts you don't know. You can sing the song when I'm not in the car." Sometimes, I purposely and subconsciously blocked out the words of the songs exactly as written. The lyrics of country and rock and roll love songs do not always reveal the truth about relationships; they hide the truth, covering it up with mostly male fantasies or romantic clichés. Rap music is even worse. It is about bad relationships, self-loathing, having no hope, everything turns to shit, and on and on and on. Most rap singers sound like fast-talking auctioneers trying to make a fast dollar.

My daughter did listen to some cool rock and roll songs, not that I understood what "cool" is anymore, discoveries passed on to the new younger generation. Usually, I would submit to my daughter's wishes of not singing and I would keep quiet. Nevertheless, secretly, I wanted to memorize all the words and sing at the top of my lungs, with the windows rolled down, at the busiest intersection in the city, with a microphone plugged into the cigarette lighter and linked to satellite speakers on the moon. I hope that at this busiest intersection, my daughter's closest friends (the ones that already drive) would pull up in their car, next to us. My daughter, Amanda, and her friends, would listen to me sing all the words to the entire song and at the end, my daughter would probably proclaim, "Dad, I hate you." To think this way is just a fantasy because no father wants to hurt the feelings of his daughter; he just wants her to understand the madness behind his purposeful ways.

Hopefully, Amanda will not become the kind of driver who brushes her hair, talks on the cell phone, puts on makeup, reads a book, plays music CDs, eats junk food, changes clothes, tidies up the car, or does all these things while at the same time driving, occasionally stopping to put a hand or two on the steering wheel. When she is driving solo and wherever she goes without me, a father just wants his daughter to be safe.

As recently as fifteen years ago, if a person wanted to make a telephone call while out on the road, he or she found a pay phone and made a local call for twenty-five cents. You added more change for long-distance calls, but at least your car remained parked and you were not a distraction to other drivers. Some states are considering laws to ban this culture of text messaging and talking on a cell phone while driving a motor vehicle. This would cause many drivers to change their ways or start getting tickets, and the roads would be much safer for everyone or so we hope.

On August 29, 2009, Missouri passed a law that makes it illegal to send text messages if you are driving a vehicle and you are twenty-one years old or younger. The new law has people shaking their heads and asking questions. How will a police officer figure out if a person is texting or dialing a cell phone and how will he know the driver's age? Does a twenty-two-year-old operate a cell phone and a steering wheel better than a twenty-one-year-old? A person's mind is distracted when talking on a cell phone, so it is impossible to imagine that a person can drive well while texting on a cell phone.

When I look at my daughters, I see the people they are. Admittedly, I sometimes see the people I think they ought to be. If it were possible, should those people meet, they would gain a completely new perspective. More importantly, most parents (the ones that care) just want their kids to stay on the right track, stay safe, be happy, be successful, and be good people.

On the day before Christmas Eve in 1997, it was difficult trying to keep Allison and Cynthia busy, as they were anxiously preoccupied with thinking about Christmas. Allison was now six years old and Cynthia, her friend who lived across the street, was eight years old. In hopes of keeping the two of them entertained and getting them out of the house, inviting them to take a hike on the jogging trail in our neighborhood seemed like a good idea. The trail was managed by the St. Louis County Parks and Recreation Department. Within minutes, we were walking down the path on the steep hill behind our house. Though the temperature was chilly, the sun was shining, two inches of snow covered the ground, and it was perfect weather for a scavenger hunt while hiking.

Asking each of the girls the same question, "Do you believe in Santa Claus?" Allison answered, "I don't know."

Cynthia replied, "Mr. Hubele, I am in the third grade and have been told that there is no Santa Claus."

This short dialogue set the scene for our scavenger hunt on the day before Christmas Eve. After talking and walking for several minutes, we came upon our first clue, a telephone pole stationed at the bottom of the hill. Gazing up at the pole, we noticed a steel plate with a large number 1 etched on it attached to the old, weathered telephone pole. "Girls, this is proof that Santa has left his mark here, because the number 1 represents the address at the North Pole," I said, the girls not seeming at all interested in my explanation.

We entered the jogging trail and continued on our way. The excitement of Christmas was in the air and we were getting exercise as my daughter was enjoying the company of her friend even more. However, where is proof of the existence of Santa Claus? If we could not find it, at least trying to find it might make this experience fun for the girls.

On the east side of Grant's Farm, the trail runs parallel to Gravois Creek. Near Grant's Farm, a gravel sandbar extends out several hundred feet across from the water in some sections. Speaking directly to the girls, I said, "The sandbar is probably the place where Santa and his reindeer rested last night." Allison giggled and Cynthia rolled her eyes. At this point, not making much progress, we needed more evidence. We continued our walk westward.

Within a few more minutes, we spotted a torn piece of red cloth clinging to a branch of a bare thorn bush. Once again trying to be convincing, "Santa must have torn part of his jolly red suit." This time, the girls listened to my explanation, but still they did not seem overly amused by my suggestions that Santa really did recently pass through our neighborhood. We continued farther along, just breathing the fresh brisk air and enjoying the outdoors, the quiet atmosphere, the snow-covered landscape, the beautiful scenery, the sounds of the wind blowing through the tall trees in the woods. By this time, we had wandered almost two miles away and that meant that we should probably think about soon turning back for home. Suddenly, in a gust of wind, a piece of clear-colored cellophane from a candy cane and a chocolate chip cookie wrapper appeared in front of our eyes. I once again explained the scenario to the girls, "After preparing to deliver presents in the neighborhood, Santa took a break and ate a snack. Do you wonder if anyone left a glass of milk for Santa, to go along with the chocolate chip cookie?"

In the near distance, we could see the bridge overpass where the train crossed on top and the walkers and bicyclers traveled underneath on the trail. This was the furthest point on the trail we could go without being required to cross a major four-lane road with lots of traffic, so we decided to turn back for home. Nevertheless, before we ventured back, my comment to the girls was, "Girls, before we get home, you can expect to come across at least one more of the clues that will prove the existence of Santa Claus."

It was evident that the girls were starting to get tired and hungry, so we turned back and started walking toward home. We only walked a few steps, when off in the distance, we could hear the whistle sounded by the train engineer. The train was creeping closer and was soon to travel across the bridge overpass, the landmark on the trail where we had just decided to turn around for home. What followed next was hard to believe on the day before Christmas Eve. As we turned and looked to see the train coming, we read the letters "S-A-N-T-A" painted on the lead train engine as it traveled across the overpass right in front of our eyes. Surely, the large letters were supposed to read "SANTA FE," but the FE part faded away from weather, or did it? Pointing and motioning for the girls to read the big letters on the side of the train, Allison and Cynthia got very excited and began holding hands and jumping up and down.

Allison said, "Dad, I was not sure about Santa Claus, but now I believe in Santa Claus for sure."

Cynthia said, "Mr. Hubele, I change my mind, that gave me goose bumps, I believe in Santa Claus too."

With newfound vigor and enthusiasm, Allison and Cynthia could not stop talking about Santa Claus, presents, and the meaning of Christmas. When we arrived home, we made hot chocolate. As we sat at the kitchen table and talked some more, the hot chocolate seemed to taste better this year.

You miss 100 percent of the chances you never take. That is but one of the pearls of wisdom, and while it might seem obvious, it is a truth we often forget about some days. Just think of the walk you never took, the job you never applied for, the stock you never purchased, the novel you never finished, the person you never asked to the dance. It happens to all of us; we get doubtful or we get too busy to smell the roses. We send many thanks to Santa Claus for delivering us a very special Christmas!

In September of 1998, my youngest daughter, Allison, at the age of seven, had just started the second grade. As usual, the first few days were all about getting the students situated and used to being back at school after the long summer vacation. The kid's first assignment was to write a short story about any subject, just so the teacher could get a feel for what the children were thinking. Here is the funny story written by Allison, with no correction to spelling, grammar, or punctuation.

Allison Hubele
264 Hillbrook Manor Drive
Fenton, MO 63026
September 2, 1998

Dear Tooth Fairy,

I just lost a tooth. I lost my tooth at school. It was so loooose, when I wigeled my tooth it just fell out. It fell on the ground. I looked on the ground but I just could not find it. I was so mad. When I got home, I asked my mom if she could take me to school, and we found it. The castodian sweeped up my tooth and saved it for me. Please give me a dollar. Thank you.

Love
Allison

Later in the same school year, 1998, Allison and I watched the movie *Field of Dreams* for the umpteenth time. Every time we watch the movie, there seems to be additional lessons about fatherhood, father-son relationships, and father-daughter relationships. We watch with appreciation as Kevin Costner tells baseball and real-life stories to his wife and daughter. "If you build it, they will come." With these words, Iowa farmer Ray Kinsella, played by actor Kevin Costner, inspired by a voice he hears to pursue a dream, builds a baseball field in the middle of a cornfield near his house. He is supported by his wife Annie, played by clever actress Amy Madigan, as he turns his property into a place where dreams can come true. Along the way, farmer Ray meets semiretired political author Terence Mann, played by celebrated actor James Earl Jones; short-term ball player, fulltime doctor, Doc Graham, played by distinguished actor Burt Lancaster; and the famous baseball player "Shoeless" Joe Jackson, played by Ray Liotta, of the Black Sox era. This movie is very heartwarming and causes you to remember loved ones who are no longer with us. Lessons in the movie teach us about following your dreams and working toward passionate goals that make you happy.

We rented this movie from the local Blockbuster Video, just one mile away from our house. But as we were about to watch this time, before the movie even began, the widely accepted FBI copyright law, as it normally does at the start of most rented VCRs or DVDs, appeared on the television screen. Occurring at the same time of this copyright screen, the following conversation took place between my seven-year-old daughter, Allison, and me.

> Dad: Every time we rent a movie, we see this same message. Allison, do you know what FBI stands for?
> Allison: Oh Dad, of course, I know what FBI stands for. We have watched many movies together.
> Dad: Ok, Allison, tell me, what does FBI stand for?
> Allison: FBI stands for February!

A few years passed us by, though it seemed like it had only been a few months. Today was May 19, 2004; the winds were blowing at gusts up to seventy miles per hour, the result of a heavy steady downpour since midnight. Winds that strong were very unusual in Missouri, unless there was a possibility of a tornado. Floods occurred every few years at the confluence of the Missouri and Mississippi Rivers. Super-floods occurred about every sixty-six years or so; in the last two, one in 1927 and one in 1993, the rivers overflowed their banks eight miles to the east on the Illinois side. The pictures of the two-story white Rockwell farmhouse intact floating down the rapidly rising Mississippi River making national headlines in 1993 will forever be etched in my mind.

It was now 7:15 a.m. and my daughter Allison and I had just finished eating breakfast (pulp-free orange juice, buttered toast, and Cheerios with skim milk) and getting ready for the day ahead of us. Anymore, one regular-sized box of cereal barely fed two people for breakfast, ever since companies quit filling cereal boxes to the top and started pumping air into the liner bags yet charging more even though the boxes weighed much less.

Because of the severe weather, I grabbed an umbrella from the foyer hall closet and helped my daughter walk to the corner bus stop, just three blocks up the hill from our house. A few minutes later, the Mehlville School District bus arrived at the corner location, where we were standing, under the umbrella, in the pouring rain. After the bus came to a halt and the red safety stop sign lever released, Allison stepped onto the bus and took her seat. "Hopefully," I thought, "By the time Allison arrived at school, her clothes would be dry enough for the start of her first hour math class." Immediately, I would be able to return home and change into dry clothing.

I was looking forward to getting some work done, paying some bills, invoicing my customers, cleaning up the house, changing the oil in my truck in the garage, and working on a few proposals for my parking lot sweeping company, "Lots of Curb Appeal, LLC."

I ran the administrative part of the business out of my house. At least that was my preconceived plan on how to attack the day.

As I approached the front porch of my house, walking back from the bus stop, I reached for my keys. Realizing that my keys were not in my pants pockets, it soon became very evident that my keys were still sitting on the kitchen table, next to the dirty breakfast dishes and utensils. Whenever I left the house, no matter how long I would be gone and no matter where I was going, it was a habit of mine to lock the front door. However, maybe the back door was still unlocked. Maybe, just maybe, the car doors were unlocked and the remote control activated in order to enter through the garage connected to the house. On the other hand, maybe the basement window was still open. I was wrong on all accounts. Everything was locked up; the house was totally secure. A quick look around pointed out that the neighbors' cars were gone (parents off to work) and all the kids already off to school. I could sense that I was alone in the neighborhood.

It would be another eight hours before Allison and the rest of the kids would return home from school. For the first two hours of killing time, a beagle, lying prone inside of its doghouse across the street, and myself, sitting in a green old-fashioned plastic stranded lawn chair on a six-by-six-foot front porch, felt the wind and listened to the rain hit the asphalt shingled roofs. Finally, there was a sudden break in the weather pattern, the sky was still mostly cloudy, a chill was in the air, and it looked like it would rain some more today, but it didn't.

For the next two hours, an inconvenient situation became an opportunity. Since the grounds became saturated, I decided to pick weeds by hand. By noon, my yard had never been so weed-free. This small feat was accomplished without using garden tools or dangerous chemicals harmful to the environment, just the use of my bare hands.

After exerting some energy, my stomach was starting to growl; I was getting thirsty and hungry. Oh yeah, I could not get inside the house. There would be no lunch today, and I did not have any money in my pocket to walk somewhere and get it. Remember, my wallet was sitting right next to my keys, which were right next to the dirty breakfast dishes on the kitchen table, inside the locked-up, much-secured house.

Another hour had passed, but then the mail carrier drove up in front of my mailbox to deliver the mail. My thoughts were full of hope that I would receive lots of mail today. Lots of mail meant there would be many items to open, many things to read. There were five pieces of mail and plenty of time in which to read every word inscribed on each item. I read both sides of the electric bill, but the main theme suggested that I owed the utility company ninety-seven dollars for usage last month. Another item turned out to be an application from a credit card company, boring read-between-the-lines stuff about personal history information; besides, I already had four major credit cards (MasterCard, Visa, Discover, and American Express) in a secure location. Remember, my wallet was sitting right next to my keys, which were right next to the dirty breakfast dishes on the kitchen table, inside the locked-up, much-secured house.

Today, May 19, 2004, was Allison's birthday; she became a teenager. She received a birthday card from Aunt Karen. Aunt Karen's cards were always inspiring, humorous, or both. Everyone always enjoyed getting cards from Aunt Karen because she would underline important messages and then add clever personal touches of her own to make you laugh or cry. Nevertheless, I was not able to read this card yet because it is addressed to Allison. Nevertheless, I did read the return address label. Aunt Karen's address etched indelibly in my mind, 9865 Ridge Park Drive, Arnold, Missouri, 63010.

The fourth piece of mail was an invitation to vacation at the YMCA Lodge in Potosi, Missouri. The letter stated, "Call today to make your reservations." There is plenty of family fun to experience at YMCA's Trout Lodge, located just seventy-five miles south of St. Louis near Potosi, Missouri. Trout Lodge's all-inclusive family vacation weekends make it easy to get away from it all, with lodge and cabin conveniences overlooking breathtaking Sunnen Lake. The lake has long been a favorite of canoeing, rafting, and kayaking enthusiasts. Families can enjoy archery, climbing, hiking, hayrides, horseback riding, trap shooting, rifle marksmanship, astronomy, rocketry, arts and crafts, and a whole directory of other activities. Supposedly, they spent lots of money for newly renovated guest rooms, a new eighteen-hole golf course, new trail rides, a bison ranch, organized lake activities and cave tours. Their rates included lodging, all meals, and most activities. The invitation welcomes clients to reserve a Friday and Saturday, and add Thursday or Sunday to complete a three-day stay for a total of only 159 dollars. Prices were valid for June, July, or August only. After reading and rereading this invitation several times, I was ready to make a reservation to stay the entire summer at the YMCA Lodge of the Ozarks in Potosi, Missouri. Oh yeah, I could not get inside the house to use the telephone. I could not drive to Potosi, Missouri, to make a reservation either, because my car keys were sitting right next to my wallet, which were right next to the dirty breakfast dishes on the kitchen table, inside the locked-up, much-secured house.

The fifth piece of mail was an office supplies catalog from "Viking Office Products Company," headquartered in Boca Raton, Florida. I wondered, "How often did it rain in Boca Raton, Florida?" After skimming the entire catalog, I now know more about copy paper and xerographic multipurpose paper, than I ever cared to know. Words such as; paperweight, xerographic, astro-bright, and pastel are now part of my office procurement vocabulary. I learned more information about low-cost clear ink jets, laser labels, laminators, shredders, sheet-feeders, and multifunction machines.

In approximately two more hours, Allison would be returning home on the school bus; my experience, confined to the front porch area for eight hours, was almost over. Even though those eight hours meant coping with small inconveniences, I still had the freedom of choosing how to deal with it. I was not bound to a prison cell or a hospital bed, and I was not being shot at over in Baghdad or Afghanistan. For most of us in the United States of America, we certainly should feel fortunate to be Americans and gratitude to all of our war veterans for the freedom to do what we want each day.

For the remaining two hours I had to wait for Allison's school bus, I contemplated and wrote the following about our nation's school systems:

Our great-grandparents' generation attended school in a one-room building with at least five other grades all at one time. The "greatest generation" walked five miles in the rain and snow to get to school. Baby boomers had to get a ride in order to drive five miles to the library to do homework. Today, children have to wait less than five seconds for their Web site to download so they can research their topic.

According to statistics, many Web sites proclaim the amount of information stored on the world Internet superhighway triples every year. Parents and teachers have to inspire our kids to be critical thinkers, problem solvers, and prepare them to sift out the facts, discarding misleading information. Parents and good teachers have an obligation to provide inspiration, the one commodity not found in a textbook.

In the twenty-first century, it is alarming to see how poorly we are doing overall in educating the children in our country. Two findings that I find most distressing are the apparent increasing decline of international standing as our students' progress through our educational system and the gap between low-income students and students from wealthier backgrounds. It is my belief that throwing more money at this problem, through increased taxes, is not a guaranteed fix-all answer. It all starts at home. Parents that put in the extra effort to get involved in their children's education seem to make the biggest difference in the success of elementary and secondary students. Inspiration and discipline are the most important concerns we can teach our children.

I would not mind paying higher taxes if it meant increased teacher salaries for better teachers and lower teacher-student classroom ratios. However, how much of taxpayers money actually gets spent in local school districts after filtering through the Internal Revenue Service, the Department of Education, the State Department, and other government agencies. A full-fledged recruitment effort to hire some of the best teachers in the nation at above-average salaries needs priority consideration in the St. Louis City School District. If the right people are in place and involved in the process, any project becomes a successful one.

Caring teachers with superior credentials can have a great impact on our children. It is not enough just to have knowledge of subject matter without having learned exposure to the many different available teaching strategies. Good judgment and common sense should be character requirements of teachers, but both of these traits can sometimes be very difficult to measure. The average amount spent per student, at most city public schools, is well over ten thousand dollars annually. Most rural county schools and private schools spend substantially less to educate their students. This suggests that schools with smaller class sizes that have teachers with great credentials and involve supporting parents are more important factors than just spending more money.

Without spending a lot of money, the Amish educate their children in small one-room schoolhouses in Bowling Green, Curryville, Louisiana, and Clarksville, small Missouri communities about an hour north of St. Louis.

At age sixteen, Pennsylvanian Dutch Amish children have this rite of passage to do whatever they want. Weird haircuts, strange clothes, reckless behavior, wild parties, and freedom of expression are all part of "devil's playground," the name given to describe the later teen years of the Amish children's experience. Discipline, grassroots values, religious beliefs, and horse-and-buggy ideals temporarily are on hold until later. When the young adult becomes twenty-one years of age, he or she must decide whether to return to the Amish lifestyle. This means no electricity, no fancy clothes, no car, no computer, no cell phone, and saying no to many of the modern conveniences exposed to them during their later teenage years. The Amish believe in traveling slow in horse-drawn buggies and closing down business on Sundays, and it is against their religion to have their face visible in a photograph. Some children make it through unscathed, but for others, it is a very difficult decision to have to choose one extreme or the other.

Mainstream men and men of all religious beliefs need to take a better stance against alcohol, drugs, guns, and teenage sex, if we are to accept our responsibility as fathers and not try to be only friends to our teenagers.

If we are there to talk with our children, to read to them, to show an interest in what they do everyday, to listen to their questions, and to help them when we are capable, we will be able to increase the chances that their natural intelligence and common sense will develop on its own.

Yet, I have found that in spite of my sincere and determined efforts, there are still more times than I care to mention when I continue to fail. There are challenges in parenting that are much more difficult than those at work are. After all, our children have something unique in them that we cannot fathom, and this slowly evolving self often makes them unpredictable. Sometimes, this can cause unwieldy and unfulfilling behavior by a parent. As parents, we feel terrible when our actions fall short and anguish when our children's actions fall short.

Back to the bus stop, at 2:30 P.M., as usual, after a short fifteen-minute ride home, the neighborhood children stepped off the school bus. The sun was shining now and I was standing at the bus stop to greet Allison as she hopped off the bus. I told her, "I love you, 'Happy Birthday, Allison,' stay safe, respect other people, and appreciate your freedom." Though she looked at me with suspicion, she did not question my remarks and after a slight pause, she said, "I love you, too."

The memories remain.

Allison received her driver's license in the summer of 2007. For almost a year, whenever she would drive, her mom or dad would ride in the car with her. After gaining a year's worth of experience, the oldest family car, an eight-year-old Honda Passport became her ride. One day, about six months after taking over possession of the Honda, Allison informed me that every time she made a right turn driving the Honda Passport, a grinding noise ricocheted throughout the car.

Driver's education classes taught Allison to pull over and park the car if she noticed loud funny noises or glowing warning lights on the dashboard circuitry. Informed of the loud grinding noise, we immediately took a test drive in our subdivision to try to diagnose the problem. Driving around in the subdivision, making mostly right turns, the grinding noise became very evident and seemed to emanate from inside the right front wheel well. Drawing from previous experiences dealing with car problems, I was sure the trouble stemmed from a faulty electronic sensor or a steering column malfunction.

Since it happened to be a Sunday, we parked the Honda in the driveway for the day, until we were able to drive the car to Gravois Auto Repair for service the next day.

The next morning, Monday, we arrived early at the repair shop to avoid the rush of people needing an abundance of car repair services. Trying to be a good example to my daughter and teaching her the important lesson of maintaining a good running vehicle, we talked to the service manager, with Allison mostly listening to our comments.

With much confidence, we went on to explain the grinding noise and the location of the problem, certain that the problem seemed related to a faulty electronic sensor or a malfunctioning steering column. The service manager entered this information into the computer and asked for the ignition keys to the eight-year-old Honda Passport. He said, "Someone will call if they have any major concerns out of the ordinary needs for parts or labor and when the car is fixed and ready to be picked up."

Since the Gravois Auto Repair shop was located across from the main entrance to our subdivision, the short walk to return home took only ten minutes. Upon unlocking the front door and entering our house, the telephone began to ring. Answering the phone on the third ring and avoiding the answering machine message to begin playing, the person on the other end identified himself as the service manager at Gravois Auto Repair. The service manager said, "Your car is ready, you can pick it up at your convenience." I answered, "That was fast; we will be there in approximately ten minutes." Thinking to myself, I wondered, "How could they fix our car so fast?"

So we headed back and after making the ten-minute return walk to Gravois Auto Repair, the service manager was waiting for us at the front counter of the service lounge area. After greeting us, he said, "Your car is ready and here are your ignition keys; the repair is on us." He then presented me with a mud flap and went on to explain, "The bent mud flap, partially cracked, hanging off, and rubbing against the tire fender well, caused the loud grinding noise when the car is in motion."

Slightly embarrassed, still thinking about my prediagnosis of a faulty electronic sensor or malfunctioning steering column, I accepted the damaged mud flap and thanked the service manager for his hospitality and no-charge repair. Allison accompanied me, leaving the repair shop. As we got back in the car, we started laughing until we were silly, knowing that my wrong diagnosis was the talk of the day at the Gravois Auto Repair shop. My feelings were similar to the feelings of the person who thought the disc holder on a computer was a coffee cup holder.

The memories remain.

One summer day when I was young, my dad told me that someday I would cross the generation gap. At the time, I did not know what he meant. You get to know your dad better when the weather gets warmer and you go near the refrigerator. Very different from the gay marriage issue or the Middle East crisis is the conflict that really matters: dads want their children to appreciate things.

You can love your children and accept their minor faults, because we all have them. But turning on every light switch in the house when only one person is home or standing there looking at everything inside the refrigerator for five minutes, then closing the door without grabbing anything, can cause a minor disturbance in any household in America. This disturbance is ugliest when the children that are hungry, growing, middle-school teenagers and dads that are home from work spend quality time together. When Dad finally notices, he asks, "Why are all the lights in the house turned on?" One of the kids might say, "So we can see when we go in that part of the house." This comment infuriates Dad because now he is mad about the kid's attitude, too.

Earlier in the morning, Dad paid the gas and electric bills, which cost one hundred fifty dollars and which would have been the same as a million dollars during the Depression for last month's energy usage. After paying all the bills, Dad took a trip to the grocery store and spent another two hundred dollars for food. Arriving back home from the grocery store, all the lights in the kitchen are turned on. After finishing putting all the groceries away, one of the kids opens the refrigerator door and looks in it for five minutes, with blank stares, then closes the door without getting anything and complaining that Dad did not get anything good to eat from the store. Dad starts thinking about the hard-earned money he spent to feed his unappreciative children, who did not turn off any of the lights or help put away any of the groceries. Dad tells the story about Grandpa.

"When Grandpa was in the navy, food was rationed during the war." He goes on to say, "The children in China or the starving children in Ethiopia would be glad to have our groceries."

My mom, my three sisters, my two daughters, my female dog, and all other women, for that matter, love to shop for clothes. In an ideal world, all women would be married to rich men, just so they had someone to feed their shopping habits. Women love to shop for dresses, blouses, shirts, skirts, bras, underwear, socks, pants, scarves, caps, hats, earmuffs, sweaters, jackets, coats, belts, shoes, shorts, stockings, slippers, boots, and sandals. Anything made out of sewn material qualifies as a product that a woman needs and qualifies as a reason for a woman to shop: pillows, curtains, rugs, carpeting, drapes, sheets, bedspreads, blankets, slipcovers, placemats, wrapping paper, awnings, upholstered furniture, and golf club covers. This list is just a small fraction of the items women will bring back from shopping trips. If manufacturers of big oil containers became privy to the idea of designing bright colorful fancy patterns on their one-quart cans and plastic bottles, it is highly probable that women would buy enormous amounts of motor oil, breaking all records for most units sold of any item made in the world.

On one shopping trip, my mom and my sisters brought home a new chair for Dad. He loved it a little too much. This chair was the best most comfortable chair for watching television, a chair fit for a king, an oversized brown suede recliner with a long cherry handle to work the footrest. When my sisters were old enough to date—sixteen or older—and a young man arrived to pick one of them up, Dad did not like it if the guy came in the front door and sat in his chair, especially if he did not introduce himself first and pass an impossible test that did not have any right answers.

When the day ended though, happy sitting in his chair, Dad had hope for another day, hope that his children learn valuable lessons, lessons they will pass along to their children when they someday cross the generation gap.

The memories remain.

The year 2005 marked my first Father's Day without my dad. Even though I saw him grow weaker for several months during the previous summer, Dad handled his battle with cancer as a true champion, never complaining.

In his later years, his dealings as an insurance executive and retirement planning whiz past, a bit of golf and lots of time hanging out at the Eat-Rite diner were his mainstays during the day. I found it comforting to know he and Mom would usually be at their home whenever I decided to visit.

Old age and a battle with cancer toppled him from his throne and now my three sisters and I must serve as tour guides of life to our own children.

When my dad died, I remember the steady stream of people who waited in long lines to pay their condolences at the funeral home. Relatives, friends from work, neighbors, patrons of the golf course, church members, retired buddies, retirees from the Veterans Association, comembers of the Elks Chapter, and hundreds of people I did not know came, as if Dad commanded the respect of a noble jester.

I came to realize Dad was a humble and good man; he treated other people the way everyone wants to be treated.

On warm Sunday afternoons in July and August, I liked sitting at the picnic table, by his side, drinking lemonade, listening to Cardinals baseball games on the radio and talking about events of the past week. If I encouraged him, he would tell me his views on political issues or some top story of the day in the news. On occasion, we would get out the long folding plastic lawn chairs and take a nap. During my childhood years, if the Cardinals had a double-header, in between games, we took a drive to Lou's gas station on the corner of Lindbergh Boulevard and Baptist Church Road, just one mile away from home. There, Dad refueled the car and I would buy two red pops from the soda machine, using the two dimes Dad gave me. Sometimes, Lou, the owner of the Sinclair gas station, if he was not too busy working on a car, threw in a couple free sodas, mainly because he liked my dad.

At times, my three sisters and I took Dad for granted. We thought, "Dad is always there when you need him." Oh, for those long, lazy Sunday afternoons during the summer, hanging out with Dad, listening to the voices of Harry Carey and Jack Buck broadcasting the baseball games on the radio in the backyard as if no one else can do it.

Observing my dad in his later years, I knew I needed to be more patient with whatever life brought me. I felt a sense of pride knowing I belonged to him. In the end, the mere presence of my dad is what I miss the most.

The memories remain.

Allison, my baby daughter, is all grown up now. She works, goes to school, tutors second-graders as a community service volunteer, and thinks for herself. On September 13, 2007, during junior year in high school, she wrote an article for English class. Her assignment was to write an article answering, "What does freedom in America mean to you today?" Knowing her as a person and that she has a strong interest in journalism makes me proud to be her father. Here is the article she wrote, titled "America Today."

> America, a melting pot where people from all places come together, represents a place of freedom. America is a place to call home and a place for everyone to feel safe no matter who he or she is or where he or she comes from. It is a place for people to find jobs and start a new beginning.
>
> Americans value a lot partly because our ancestors made the decision to have a constitution and be a free country a long time ago. America has been through so much. There has been time to grow and learn from our mistakes. In spite of war and natural disasters, America became stronger, proving we can handle a lot and still stay strong through it all.
>
> Americans all need to make a living. Money is what makes the world go round. Americans strive to achieve productive careers. Whether as a doctor, teacher, writer, plumber, or a fast-food worker, everyone needs to make a living. Some people go to college to study their majors; others take a break from school and learn on the job. Some graduate and some do not. Everyone has choices to make. As an American, you have many rights, but some people abuse their privileges.

America is not perfect. America has a problem with letting anyone come into our country and it takes a legal process to become an American citizen. In some of the foreign places people come from, Americans would be in danger in their country. It is as if people from different parts of the world are coming to the United States as a last resort to get away from terrorism and barbaric rulers. When they come here, the first thing they should do is learn English, if they do not know it already.

America relies on imports such as gas, oil, crops, cars, leather, fabrics, jewels, steel, and iron ore from other parts of the world. Sweatshops overseas pay men and women, even children, to make products and ship them to the United States. They pay them so little for their hard work, and then owners have the right to sell the products to American customers for five times the costs to make the product. United States government officials have taken some steps trying to enforce trade regulations to try to fix this problem.

Another issue that is a big problem is people not adjusting to diversity. There are so many different kinds of people living in the United States, and the world should be used to it by now. I think parents and grandparents forget that it is the year 2007 and pass bad habits to their kids and grandkids. They are so biased and racist that they do not want to change, and that is the reason society is still like it is, giving special rights just because that is not the way it has always been.

Women's rights have gained a lot over the years, but the issue still is not perfect. We still have not had a woman president, which soon may change. One has run for vice-president and one is currently running for president. In the past, women, treated like dirt, had no rights. Women stayed home, cleaned, and cooked. From my point of view, women still do not have all the rights men do. Everyday I see it; whether it is sociably or verbally; they talk with rude and unnecessary comments. Think about it. If you were still a kid on a playground, playing kickball, and girls are treated second class.

America, its children, adults, the elderly, people with disabilities, people that have their health, must stand for equality. It is everyone being brought together and celebrating what we have: patriotism. Some people express their feelings and go all out; some people keep their feelings to themselves; but no matter what, everyone has it. If they did not, they would not live here. America is beautiful and America is free. Everyone should respect the place we call home.

"America Today," written by Allison Hubele

Living in the Midwest, working, and raising children in this great country called the United States of America, my family, including my two grown daughters, is fortunate to live in a place where we are able to express our opinions freely and intelligently, either verbally or by the written word. It is a proud moment on a day such as this, when a parent realizes one of their children has reached a place; where they have grown so much as an individual to eloquently write how they feel. There is much hope for future generations.

Allison graduated from Mehlville High School on her birthday, May 19, 2009. During the graduation ceremonies, the principal talked about how the graduates should continue to work hard and make a difference in the world. The Chairman of the Board of Education announced the scholarship winners, and as Allison received her diploma, he announced, "Allison Hubele is the recipient of the A-plus two-year scholarship and will be attending St. Louis Community College."

Many of the memories of such wonderful and challenging moments of fatherhood remain.

"GOLF AND FISHING"

This is a legendary story about a golfer who swore off the game for good. There are similar forms and shapes of this legend told and retold wherever golfers gather, but I actually witnessed this event.

In April 1966, at the age of twelve, golf was an enticing but new sport. I was just trying to learn and get better playing the game. Though relatively new to the game of golf, I joined Dad and his coworkers at the annual company golf outing. I will never forget a golfer, Train Trammel, who went by the nickname "Gunner"—at least that is what his fellow golfing friends called him. He worked at an office building on West Florissant Avenue in Florissant, Missouri, the same one my dad drove to everyday for the past ten years. I was not sure how he obtained this nickname, maybe because he plays a fast game or he gunned it while stepping on the gas pedal of the golf cart driving on the cart path as if a train moves swiftly on the railroad tracks.

Gunner was in the leading foursome and the first golfer to tee off at the first hole. My dad and I, along with two of Dad's coworkers, waited to follow them when the "starter" called our names.

Gunner did some easy stretches to warm up, took a few practice swings, teed his golf ball, and declared he was ready to address the ball. He took a full swing and hit his drive into the middle of the lake. Upset over his bad shot, he threw his entire bag of clubs into the water and started walking back to his car. One swing and he was done. Watching in disbelief, I overheard his friends say his sets of golf clubs are brand new; he just bought them.

Appearing to reconsider the situation, Gunner came walking back, took off his shoes, and with his pant legs rolled up to his knees, waded into the murky water. He retrieved his golf bag and pulled it out of the hallowed muddy basin of the lake. Subsequently unzipping a pocket on the side of the golf bag, he pulled out his car keys, then threw his golf bag, clubs still intact, back into the water, walked to his car and drove home. The lake had a reputation for swallowing golf balls, but most victims continued to navigate the course and enjoy their round, whether they shot par or barely broke one hundred, at least they finished. Apparently, this morning started out as a brutal beginning to the day for this man with a bad temper, possessed by the burden of the beast.

The memories remain.

People of all ages play golf and the social aspect of the game improves your mood. Most people work so hard and seldom take time out to smell the roses, caught up in the demands of their daily lives. Sometimes just a walk in the woods or a round of golf can put harmony back in your life.

Every Saturday morning during the summer of 1988, three of my closest friends and I played golf. At sunrise, our foursome had the first tee time. Playing golf at Sunset Lakes Golf Course, a moderately priced golf course located on West Watson Road in St. Louis, Missouri, was a special treat that we always enjoyed. For thirty-four dollars per person, foursomes were able to play eighteen holes and share two electric riding carts, and golfers were told to keep the carts on the asphalt pathways. This links-style course had five lakes that come into play on nine of the eighteen holes. The greens are well maintained, slightly undulating, well-manicured and some multi-tiered. The signature hole is the par-five number six, featuring a very scenic flowing creek and a lake in front of an elevated bent grass green.

Dad worked behind the counter and was in charge of signing up golfers and making sure things ran smooth in the pro shop. He had a wonderful way with people, the golfers liked him, but it was also a great way that he could supplement his retirement income and have a good time too.

On the first Saturday in June of 1988, just getting started, Mark Bigley elected to be the first one in our group to hit his tee shot. Bigley was a good athlete and usually considered a good golfer, but not on this day. As the rest of us—Tom Wildcat, Dick Ohshit, Gene Holdover, and I—watched, Bigley's drive off the first tee hit a tree that was located approximately thirty yards to the right of the tee box. The golf ball ricocheted back toward where all of us were standing. In an instant, Bigley reached out and caught his golf ball. The three of us were so stunned that none of us said a word. Bigley subsequently placed his golf ball back on the tee and then he proceeded to power drive his second attempt 295 yards straight down the middle of the fairway.

After a brief stint of laughter, we pondered the ruling of this unusual circumstance. The four of us (excluding Bigley in our fivesome), agreed that the golf ball lies seven, three strokes for hitting an extra drive and adding a penalty stroke, one stroke penalty for touching the ball, one stroke penalty for moving or impeding the flight of the ball, and one stroke penalty for hitting ball out of bounds. Bigley disagreed. "Because the ball stayed in flight pattern the entire time, eventually rolling to a stop in the middle of the fairway, the golf ball lays one," said Bigley not so convincingly, but in his unique and humorous way.

The memories remain.

Sunset Lakes Golf Course lies on the historic laden flatlands next to the foggy banks of the Meramec River. "The Shawnee Indians were the first to settle on the banks of the Meramec River. Missouri joined the Union in 1821. William Clark, on behalf of the United States and delegates from the Shawnee Nation, signed the Treaty of St. Louis on November 7, 1825. In this treaty, the Shawnee ceded lands to the United States, lands south from St. Louis to Cape Girardeau. In return for the land, the United States government gave the Shawnee a sum of eleven thousand dollars and leased to them a blacksmith shop for five years providing all tools and 300 pounds of iron annually." [4]

After the Treaty of St. Louis lease expired, the United States government forcibly relocated the Missouri Shawnees to southeastern Kansas, close to the Neosho River. Today, the largest part of the Shawnee nation resides in Oklahoma.

Besides enjoying the game, talking to other golfers teaches you about the history of the land and the river that flows next to the Sunset Lakes Golf Course. Reading books from the Oklahoma State University library helps verify the information.

Sometimes golfers talk about history and sometimes they talk about the perfect golf swing, the one that allowed you to score a hole-in-one. The golf swing is about demonstrating control and letting go all at the same time—what a perfect metaphor for life. Do not hit it left, do not hit it right, do not hit it long, do not hit it short, and you will be all right. What is more exciting than hitting one shot and marking the number one on your golf scorecard? Tom Morris scored the first professional ace on the eighth hole at Prestwick Country Club during the British Open in 1869. Tiger Woods has eighteen aces, the first when he was just eight years old. Elsie McLean, the oldest person on record, had to wait until she was 102 years old to make a hole-in-one. In a span of just two hours, Nick Price, Jerry Pate, Doug Weaver, and Mark Wiebe all scored ones on the sixth hole at Oak Hill Country Club during the 1989 U.S. Open.

Everyday, during the golfing season in St. Louis, usually from April through to the end of October, the *Post-Dispatch* newspaper reports the area golf results. On Sunday, June 11, of that same remarkable year, the year of the 1989 U.S. Open, the newspaper listed the names of local people who had a hole-in-one on the previous day. On Saturday, June 10, 1989, Steve Hubele, using an eight-iron, had a hole-in-one on the 133-yard number seven hole at Sunset Lakes Golf Course. One week later, on June 17, 1989, George Hubele (Dad), using a six-iron from 135 yards away, had a hole-in-one on the same number seven hole at Sunset Lakes Golf Course.

The very next week, on Saturday, June 25, 1989, Dad and I played in a charity fundraising tournament at Sunset Lakes. After playing our way through the first six holes, as we walked our way toward the seventh tee, we noticed a brand-new Lincoln automobile sitting next to the green. A representative from the Hilltop Lincoln-Mercury car dealership was sitting on the side of the hill next to the car. The representative, named Cindy, was there to watch in case any golfer made a hole-in-one during the tournament, because if they did, they would win the car. Our friends, Mark Bigley and Tom Wildcat, were the other two golfers in our foursome. Bigley and Wildcat, with heightened enthusiasm, told the representative that Dad and I each had a hole-in-one in previous weeks.

After waiting a few minutes for the group in front of us to finishing putting, it was our turn to hit tee shots on the number seven hole. I went first, using an eight-iron, of course, the same iron used for my hole-in-one, and drove the ball into the middle of the small lake in front of the green. Dad was next. Using a seven-iron, of course, the same iron he used for his hole-in-one, he drove the ball almost to the green, but it hit the side of the hill and rolled back into the lake. Like father, like son, our shots ended up in the water, but we had a few laughs and enjoyed the day together. Oh, if the holes-in-one would have just come a week or two later.

After we finished our rounds of golf, we retired to the clubhouse for sandwiches and drinks. Dad told a story. "Three of the groundskeepers contracted to paint the wood siding on our clubhouse here at the golf course. Being frugal, they bargain-shopped and scrimped to spend as little as possible on paint and materials. When the three men were halfway finished with the job, they determined that they did not have enough paint to finish their work. They decided to dilute the water-based paint in order to stretch its coverage, to finish the job. They diluted the paint a couple more times, causing the paint to become streaky and run as the color of the paint became a lighter shade each time. As the three men had just about finished painting the last corner section near the apex of the roof, all of the sudden the sky thickened with clouds and down poured the rain. The paint smeared even worse and large air bubbles formed on the wooden siding of the clubhouse. A voice raged down from the heavens, 'Repaint, you thinners. Repaint, and thin no more.'"

Dad's stories and jokes were funny and he always gave a piece of himself when he talked to you. He gave his best effort to brighten a stranger's day.

The memories remain.

On the course, many of my friends had some of the same flaws in their game: a tendency toward self-delusion, competing in a state of darkness, an addiction to playing golf, groveling, hardheadedness, and a general preoccupation with sports. Charles Darwin, in analyzing golfers, may have been able to explain why we are who we are and why we do what we do. However, it was his grandson, Bernard Darwin, who wrote about Ben Hogan and Gene Sarazen during the early years of golf. Older golf fans can remember Ben Hogan walking up the eighteenth fairway with a slight limp and a grimace on his face; maybe watching Johnny Miller making six birdies in a row. Certainly, they remember the shock of Larry Mize's pitch-in to beat Greg Norman in the Masters Championship. Not many people know about the day Hogan and the boys met the senior golfers and the squirrel. Here is how the story unraveled:

On another hot day, late in the summer of 1988, playing golf with good friends—Homer Hogan, a package goods delivery driver; Spider Derski, a lieutenant for a local metropolitan police department; and Mark Bigley, a manager for a large printing company—seemed like a good idea. Yes, this is the same Mark Bigley in the previous golf outing story.

We all met in the parking lot at Forest Park Golf Club, a popular public golf course in the central-west end of the city of St. Louis, Missouri. This picturesque twenty-seven-hole course has a lot of history and it was built on the sight of the 1904 World's Fair, but we were about to make some of our own history. The course had been rearranged and the clubhouse remodeled several times in past decades. The course sits in the middle of historic Forest Park, and on weekends, golfers can anticipate seeing people in the park visiting the Art Museum, St. Louis Zoo, and the Science Center, roller-skating, picnicking, or walking the trails enjoying the scenery. The golf course advertises features such as two waterfalls, Zoysia grass fairways, and a great urban setting surrounded by countless numbers of one-hundred-year-old oak trees.

We had to wait approximately one hour before we could tee off. A large group of almost fifty seniors, who had signed up in front of us, was playing in a tournament. After lots of catching up with small talk and practicing our putting on the practice green, it was finally our turn on the first tee. The first nine holes played routinely for our foursome of friends. We were enjoying the weather, the scenery, and the level of golf—a smattering of bogies, a few pars and even a couple of birdies. For all practical purposes, this commemoration begins at the tee box on the tenth hole of the golf course. The scorecard listed the number ten hole as measuring six hundred yards in length and considered it the longest hole on any golf course in the St. Louis region. Locals call the tenth hole the "Skinker Monster," because the lengthy layout parallels Skinker Avenue. Known to disappear into the front grilles of cars are golf balls driven from the number ten tee-boxes.

Since I had the honor of having the lowest score on the front nine holes, it was my turn to swing first at the tenth tee box. I hit a great tee shot that stayed in the middle of the fairway and rolled to a stop almost 275 yards away. As good as my tee shot was, my second shot, using a three-wood in the fairway, was even better. It traveled 280 yards and stuck on the side of a mound just 55 yards from the flagpole. I followed those two big hits with a high-flying shot, using a pitching wedge that landed on the green, just ten feet away from the hole. As the saying goes, "So far, so good." Unfortunately, it took me four putts from ten feet away to knock the golf ball in the hole. Several of the older senior golfers, backed up from slow play and waiting at the next tee box on top of the hill, witnessed my unfortunate poor play. After driving around the green to the next hole, I parked the golf cart, walked up the hill to the next tee, and waited behind the older senior golfers. Directing his attention toward me, one of the old-timers said, "You had a little trouble putting on that green, did you not son?"

"Yes, I was on the green in regulation, in three shots, but proceeded to four-putt," I explained.

The old-timer replied, "That hole was a par five. Well, I was on the green in five and one-putted, so I beat you."

With all that said, here came this squirrel, which had run across Skinker Avenue and across the fairway, up the hill. It then positioned itself on the front seat of my golf cart. The squirrel placed its two front paws on the steering wheel and followed that feat by depositing feces on the driver's side of the front seat, astoundingly, lying in two small piles. As one might expect, the squirrel's exhibition observed by the other senior golfers and the golfers in my foursome, as all of us were waiting on the tee box at the eleventh hole. After a very brief moment of silence and with a perfect sense for timing, the old-timer uttered, "See, that was a message from God, you should have two-putted!" Laughter broke out on top of the hill of the eleventh tee box at Forest Park Golf Club on that day.

Well, each golfer in my foursome was too young, to be invited to finish play in the local senior's golf tournament, but we had a great time anyway. My friend, Homer Hogan, though he has a great golf surname, is not related to the legendary golfer "Ben Hogan." However, Homer is a gifted and knowledgeable storyteller, and for many years to come, he will be talking about this day on the old historic golf course.

The memories remain.

Smelling freshly mowed grass on a well-'groomed' golf course is part of the experience I hope for before setting out to play golf. I also envision making a bunch of pars. There is more to this game than chasing a little white ball. In one afternoon on a course, golf can remind you that most often the greatest challenges you face are against yourself. Golf can question your honesty and your character; it offers you a chance to show sportsmanship or a choice to get angry when you hit a bad shot. The game becomes a test; it mirrors life and teaches valuable lessons that go beyond the rules of the game and reveal the true nature of the human condition.

On a warm sunny weekend day in early May of 1999, my daughter Allison asked, "Dad, have you played any golf with Joe yet?" Allison knew Joe and I usually started playing golf in early May, after the spring rains, when the weather became consistently warmer. She must have extrasensory perception, because Joe had called me on the previous morning for that very reason. Joe Hacker works as a freight shipper for a large Fortune 500 corporation. At the start of each season, we would usually visit a driving range or two before scheduling a tee time at any of the local golf courses.

The next day, my friend Joe and I met at 9:00 a.m. at the Pro-Am Golf Center driving range. Founded in 1975, by Thomas D. DeGrand, Pro-Am specializes in providing the sale of golf equipment to companies in the incentive business. They also offer a fitting studio, golf club repair, and professional golf lessons at their driving range. The driving range is nestled between a gas station on one side, an urban subdivision on the other side, and tall maple and oak trees on the backside. Out front sit the pro-shop and a gravel parking lot big enough to accommodate about thirty cars. The pro-shop has a great selection of golf clubs including brands Taylor Made, Titleist, Cobra, Callaway, Cleveland, Mizuno, Nike, Hogan, and Ping, all at competitive prices.

Joe and I pulled into the parking lot of the driving range at the same time. The driving range was open for business, but the grass was still very soggy due to the heavy rains from the week before. After exchanging pleasantries, we both decided to pay the five-dollar rental fee for a large bucket of fifty range golf balls. Pro-Am advertises that their company is proud to represent the Professional Golfers Association of America by enhancing the game through quality products and instruction. They promote their ten lighted and covered tees, fifteen outside tees, and sufficient area to hit off the grass. To mirror the reality of driving the golf ball on the tee at any given golf course, we decided to buy a bag of plastic tees and hit off the grass. Neither Joe nor I preferred to drive golf balls off the Astroturf mats, because the bounce effects off the mats were too forgiving. For more or less thirty minutes, enjoying each other's conversation, Joe and I continued to hit golf balls. The mood of the day would change with my next swing of the golf club.

The club attendant stationed Joe and me approximately fifteen feet apart on the grass at the end of the driving range property, and I stood positioned to the right of Joe. Further to the right, another fifteen feet away, a lofty chain-link fence divided compartmentalized sections of the Pro-Am Golf Center driving range. Up to this point, each of us had hit about thirty shots apiece. Feeling warmed up and energetic, I proceeded to take a full swing at my next tee shot, using a Big Bertha driver. In an instant, I heard two sounds, a "clank," followed by a "splat." I had not picked up the flight of the golf ball to follow its path. As I immediately looked over my left shoulder, I noticed Joe buckled over in a slumped position. His eyes were bugged out, his mouth was wide open, and both of his hands cupped over the place where the legs fork from the human body. I thought I had killed Joe.

Apparently, the golf ball ricocheted off the chain-link fence pole and struck Joe's lap with missile-like force. Worried, I responded by asking, "Joe, are you OK, where did the golf ball hit you?" At first glance, Joe could not reply, as he was still trying to catch his breath. Just a few moments later, his fear and mine subsided. Next, he relayed this funny message to me:

"I think I am going to be okay. The golf ball appeared to hit me on my inner right thigh area; it did not hit me on my testicles, though I probably will suffer from a tremendous bruise. I am even more fearful of the suffering I will endure from the repercussions from our other golfing buddies, when they hear what happened to me."

The memories remain.

During the summer months, for twenty consecutive years between 1975 and 1995, our family vacationed at Kentucky Lake or Lake of the Ozarks. Most of the time, we planned our trips around holidays, three—or four-day weekends. Without having to drive too far, it was fun to get away and relax, go fishing, socialize, and enjoy riding on a boat.

In July of 1995, my family decided to arrange a fishing trip to Kentucky Lake. Brother-in-law Mike Meyer was the first one out in a boat, fishing the coves for bluegill and bass. During the same week, unbeknownst to either of us at the time, a good friend named Jim Worths was fishing somewhere on this lake. Jim also made the two-hundred-mile trip to Kentucky Lake and stayed at a beach cabin resort with other fishing pals. Because he was excited about his recent purchase, Jim volunteered to drive this trip, pulling his brand-new Lowe fishing boat with a Mercury outboard motor sitting on back of it.

Five hours after leaving St. Louis, Jim and his friends met up at the resort. It was still early afternoon, so they eagerly decided to unpack their things and head for the nearest public boat ramp. After a short tow down a gravel road, Jim backed the trailer down the steep embankment and lowered his boat down the ramp and into the water. A few moments later, he and his friends were sitting in the boat and paddling away from the loading ramp. A large sign stated that it was a rule to drift out past the wake before starting the motor. This was a safety rule to alert boaters of swimmers and the start of the busy stages of the tourist season. Finally, they were out on the lake, the weather was gorgeous, and they could enjoy some manly conversation, or at least they thought.

They paddled and drifted out past the wake, probably fifteen hundred feet from shore. Heavy was their anticipation of riding across the lake to fish off the points. With his friends sitting in front of him, Jim was about to start the brand-new Mercury outboard motor. After he pulled the ripcord to start the engine, the motor sounded great, but within seconds, as Jim and his friends looked in disbelief, the Mercury outboard motor fell off the back end of the boat. The water was probably two hundred feet deep at this part of the lake. Somehow, during the tow from St. Louis to Kentucky Beach Resort, the boat and motor stayed connected and intact. Apparently not tightened down were the nuts and bolts that attached the motor to the boat. When Jim pulled the ripcord, this movement created enough of a jolt to force the motor to fall and sink to the bottom of the lake. Nothing they could do would get the motor back. From this experience, though they felt helpless and cheated, they were able to laugh about it.

This put a damper on the fishing trip. It took a few weeks for Jim to get over his loss. Several months later, Jim received a Christmas card from Kentucky Beach Resort. It read:

> We wish Happy Holidays to all! We wish you all the very best for the coming year and hope the year soon departing has blessed you with happiness.
>
> Improvements to the resort continue. We have come a long way since our arrival in 1985, and we still have plenty to do. This past year, the work has become more noticeable. The grounds are looking wonderfully groomed; we did some cosmetic cabin updates last winter that were badly needed, and we opened another new cabin last spring. The water tower got an overhaul and it is just beautiful up there on the hill. For those of you that were here during the spring flood, thanks for having patience. The water level peaked at the end of May and took ten days to recede. We managed to get the boat dock back in order and the swimming pool ready for summer operation. We did survive.
>
> Our darling Siamese cat, Lucky, passed away the end of May. Most of you knew him, and many of you were fond of him. His shining personality and overwhelming social ability are great memories. Memories of Lucky at the fish-cleaning station, roaming the grounds every evening for his "social

hour" with everyone, and his attempts to get someone to take him for a boat ride will live on. We will always miss him.

Once again, we look forward to seeing you this coming year, whether for a fishing trip, golf, shopping, or something else. Pack your bags, give us a call and head this way . . . We would love to see you. By the way, Jim, don't forget to tighten the bolts. Wouldn't it be nice if, whenever we messed up our life, we could simply press 'Control-Alt-Delete' and start all over? Amen, Amen!

We wish you and your families all the best this holiday season and in the years ahead.

Annie and Sam
Kentucky Beach and Spa Resort
BIG BASS COUNTRY

The memories remain.

After reaching fifty years of age, most athletes resign themselves to becoming armchair coaches and screaming meaningless advice at sporting events on television. Some try to stay active but compete in senior leagues to even out the competition. Tom Watson defied all the odds and nearly put the final touches on what would have been the greatest story in the history of golf.

The British Open is always the toughest tournament on the professional golf tour each year because the rounds of golf played on courses where golf originated are not groomed like most modern ones, and the fairways and roughs resemble cow pastures. The July 2009 British Open was so difficult that even Tiger Woods did not qualify to play the final two rounds.

On the fourth and final day of the tournament, Watson needed only a par four on the last hole to win, but his second shot took a bad bounce and went over the putting green. Instead of chipping close to the flag and one putting, he finished with a bogey five. He eventually lost the golf tournament to Stewart Cink in a four-hole playoff match.

Fifty-nine-year-old Watson played impelling golf for four straight days, and though it was a heartbreaking loss at the end, he showed us how to act with sportsmanship and class. He truly is one of the all-time golf legends, and he was one of Dad's favorites.

The memories remain.

"PAPER BOY"

One of the earliest newspapermen was Benjamin Franklin, a pioneer of journalism and the U.S. Postal Delivery Service, one of the men most responsible for the success of newspaper publishing in the early years of our country.

Today, whether you want an update on local news, ideas for weekend entertainment, or play-by-play of the latest game, you can usually find it in the *St. Louis Post-Dispatch* newspaper. The *Post-Dispatch* and the *Suburban Journals*, all owned by Pulitzer, Inc. at the end of the twentieth century, have sections featuring business, shopping, real estate, auto, and employment ads. The thirty-seven editions of the *Suburban Journals* are as diverse as the communities they serve. Stories about community government, school boards, neighborhood associations, and chambers of commerce receive high visibility in Pulitzer products. The *St. Louis Post-Dispatch* publishes obituaries, births, anniversaries, weddings, engagements, and a calendar for community groups to publicize their special events. For all the aforementioned reasons and more, many of the two-and-a-half-million residents of the St. Louis metro region depend on carriers to deliver the newspaper in a reasonable and timely fashion.

Steve Hubele Incorporated launched in 1995, with the purchase of a newspaper route in Webster Groves bordered by Laclede Station Road on the east, Watson Road on the south, Edgar Road on the west, and Florence Avenue on the north. The route, which included two thousand homes and a gated retirement community, measured twenty-five miles long and included eight hundred daily subscribers. Some days, deliveries went smoothly; other days meant delays due to printing press malfunctions or truck breakdowns bringing papers from the press to the carrier drop-site.

Like mail delivery, weather did not stop newspaper delivery. "The show must go on". Illness rarely stops newspaper carriers. If a carrier is battling the flu, he works through it because he has no other choice; no one else knows the route. It takes a special person, dedicated and disciplined, to do this kind of job. Occasionally, Dad helped roll newspapers by riding along on Sundays to help save time and relieve a little pressure on the busiest day for circulation.

There goes the "Paper Boy!" That was the message I heard repeatedly at the Laclede Groves retirement apartments. For some reason, I did not feel appreciated or respected when called "Paper Boy". I was a diligent and hard-working fifty-year-old man. I felt like the "beast of burden," usually carrying two fifty-pound bundles of newspapers at a time, up and down five flights of stairs in most of the buildings on my route delivering newspapers every night on foot to more than a thousand residents of the Webster Groves, Missouri, retirement community called Laclede Groves. Even when the night apartment manager, who was younger than me, would see me working my newspaper route, he would insist on calling me "Paper Boy".

I thought, "Why do some people have to be intentionally inconsiderate toward others. Besides, I would never think of calling a forty-seven-year-old maintenance manager names such as 'Fix-It-Boy' or 'Tinker Bell.'" Life's lessons teach us that most of the time, it is not "what you say," but "how you say it." The following letters, some finding fault and some expressing thanks, were sent to me during my working days (May 1995 through Aug 2002) as a *St. Louis Post-Dispatch* newspaper carrier.

Dear Mr. Hubele,

I regret very much my part in the shouting match that took place between us over the phone. I do not want to conduct business in that way. Your words were disrespectful to me, but I do understand that you may be bitter over customers that have been unfair to you. I did send you a notification in writing with my last payment. The *St. Louis Post-Dispatch* customer service office said they would not pursue me for payment of the unwanted papers, per my telephone conversation with them on July 23, 1998. God, the Holy God of the bible sets a different standard for those who would love him. Therefore, because of His words in James 5:4 and in spite of financial pressures here, I am sending the complete final payment out of respect for the labor that you put in to delivering the newspapers.

Sincerely,
Mrs. G. Fanthouse

Note: I never shouted at this elderly woman, do not remember ever receiving a cancellation notice, and I never cashed her check for $21.05; her letter still hangs in my office.

Dear Steve,

Please do not throw the newspaper on the grass, throw it on the driveway.

B. Rueter

Dear Steve,

Please do not throw the newspaper on the driveway, throw it on the grass.

K. Hasmuss

Dear Steve,

Young people make mistakes, too. My telephone number is 555-5646. I am almost ninety-five years old, so you might call me when I am negligent with payment. I do believe that I pay too much for the newspaper. I started taking this newspaper in 1939, when I lived on Tuxedo Avenue in Webster Groves, Missouri. I never have had any trouble getting the newspaper delivered to me. Thank you for the good service!

Mr. King Bossett

Note: Price for newspaper in 1939 was five cents each copy, price for everyday newspaper delivery in 1998 was thirty-three dollars per month.

Dear Steve,

Just to let you know that I have a definite report from my doctors; it is bone cancer and it is terminal (one day at a time), so that is why I have not seen you in a long time. I am trusting in the Lord. I also have nurses that provide hospice care and all of the equipment for me to stay at home. Have a great summer; God bless you and your family.

Mrs. Miller

Note: Mrs. Miller was such a nice woman; she always sent me a gratuity with her payment each month and even a bigger gratuity at Christmastime. Even when suffering from cancer, she took the time to write me and bless my family. Mrs. Miller died three months after sending me this letter.

Dear Steve,

It would help if you enclosed a self-addressed stamped envelope with the bill!

Grace W.

Dear Steve,

You want me to pay you immediately, but you send me a bill once every month. I should make you wait a month.

P. Moore

Dear Steve,

Please deliver the Sunday newspaper to me on Monday.

Note: This letter had no name or return address.

Dear Steve,

Did you ever read a wrinkled wet newspaper? Please, the name is Daeger.

Dear Steve,

I suggest that you double-bag the newspapers. Blue—and red-colored bags would be nice and a white twister used to tie the bags.

Vern

Note: I suspect that Vern was a World War II veteran. This is a nice idea but if I did this, I would have never been able to get all eight hundred newspapers delivered in a timely fashion. The Post-Dispatch wanted all newspapers delivered between 2 a.m. and 6 a.m.

Dear Steve Hubele,

I have found active water bugs in my newspapers! We do not want to get them started in our apartments. Please attend to this matter at this time!

Mrs. C. W.

Note: This customer's newspaper was one of a stack of newspapers bundled and brought inside and placed on the floor in the lobby area. Most likely, a water bug can get inside anytime the entrance door opened. However, after receiving this letter, I started placing newspapers on a table inside lobby area.

Dear Steve,

Some people are complaining about having to pay for the newspaper; it should be free.

L. W. M.

Dear Paper Boy,

Cancel my newspaper subscription. I am an eighty-year-old and have very poor eyesight. Stock market quotes are in such small print, I cannot even read it with my magnifying glasses. In addition, newspaper deliveryman arrives at about 4:00 a.m. when it rains the hardest. For the last two weeks, newspapers were sopping wet when I finally woke-up at noon. It took another week to dry them. Check, dated 8/1/98 enclosed for twenty-one dollars and thirty-one cents; I deducted for wet newspapers.

J. H. L.

Dear Steve,

   Watch out for the Chicago Cubs, next World Champs! My wife says I have a hole in my head where my brain should be.

Mr. Pratton

Note: Mr. Pratton was a retired manufacturers' representative. He would be drinking his coffee early in the morning and would be waiting to open the door for me as I was carrying bundles of paper on each arm. We both enjoyed the game of baseball and had a good time ribbing each other about the rivalry. He was very knowledgeable on many fronts and was one of the kindest people I've ever met.

Dear Steve,

   I still have not received credit for the one Saturday paper when I went out of town for the day. I did not want to get the paper delivered on that day. Please credit my account thirty cents.
   Apartment #1535

Note: This letter came from the same man in his thirties, while standing on his front porch in a ten-inch snowstorm and watching me deliver newspapers on foot. He said, "Unbelievable that we get our newspaper today; we have the best delivery carrier in the world."

Dear Post-Dispatch:

The person who sees to it that our newspapers are on the driveway when we get up each day is deserving of a special thank you. He delivers everyday, including holidays, weekends, snow, rain, or sleet. I believe he is deserving of a job-well-done award.

                                            Anonymous

Dear Steve,

Thank you for your fine service over the years, but please note the following message. I just want to tell you about our new little dog, "Patches." She is quite a barker and when anyone is on our property, the hackles on her back sort of stand up. She is a two-year-old Mexican Chihuahua with Beagle mix. Once, she bit a child at the daycare center down the street. However, once she gets to know you, she just barks until someone pets or talks to her. You will grow to love her.

Dear Steve Hubele and family,

We previously sent a "holiday gift check" for your family; however, by mistake we inserted the check with the electric bill. I am sorry this happened, but with Christmas and being so busy, we just want to send our blessings.
Thank you,

                        Mr. and Mrs. Mitchum and Dog Peaches

Note: Never did receive "holiday gift check". Mr. and Mrs. Mitchum sure could make you laugh. The electric company never mailed me the check.

Dear Mr. Steve Hubele,

Please tell your supplier to avoid rumpling up the newspapers. All sections were messed up this morning. It makes the start of the day difficult.

Harold R.

Dear Mr. Hubele,

Enclosed is my check. Since you took over the paper route, the quality of the service is declining. In the past, the newspaper generally arrived by 4:00 a.m. or earlier. Now it arrives at 4:05 a.m. or 4:10 a.m. I hope you can improve the service. I am a loyal subscriber, but I want the paper by 4:00 a.m.
Thanks,

John B. "Old Westbury"

Note: We live in a society that has what I call the "McDonald's Hamburger" mentality. We want cheerful service and we do not want to wait for it. Even though it meant slightly increased gasoline expenses, I changed the pattern of my route to accommodate the customer. Even with the change, John was waiting at the curb with his flashlight at 4:00 a.m. My timely service was important to him. Later on, I found out that Mr. John B. was a stockbroker and he needed an early jump on the market to do his job.

Dear "Paper Boy,"

After speaking with you on the telephone, about where and why I wanted my newspaper thrown on my driveway, everything was fine during the months of July and August. Almost everyday in August, my newspaper landed in the wrong square in the driveway. On the rainy Sunday of August 18, you even managed to hit the very spot I had warned you my paper would get wet . . . and it did! The open sleeve was toward the garage door and the water ran down and into the paper. This is what I am going to do for every time my paper is not within two feet, two inches from my front door . . . I will not pay for it!

Betty S.

(Six years later, I received the following letter from the same woman)

Dear "Paper Boy,"

Sorry you are leaving to pursue a different career. Once I "straightened you out" on where to throw my newspaper, you gave me wonderful delivery service. However, I hate that we have only one major newspaper in this town and it is so liberal. It is like electricity, gas, and water . . . What other choice do we have?

Betty S.

Steve,

Have you ever thought of having your customers pay your bank? I have no idea what the bank would charge as a collection agency or how cost efficient that would be with your present operation. It could expedite your cash flow. Computers work wonders these days. Maybe the bank could even bill your customers; but that might be too expensive. Surely, "cash flow" must be important to you in the early stages of taking over a paper route business. I am anxious for you to succeed. I am not opposed to your two-month billing cycle, but it would seem to me that it would be easier to keep track of cancellations and vacations during a one-month billing cycle. I am not in any way trying to tell you how to operate, but I used to volunteer and still have an interest in seeing that small businesses succeed. These are just some thoughts.

Regards,
Ralph C. 11/7/96

Note: Ralph C. had many good ideas and a very sharp mind for a man in his nineties.

There is pride in doing something for other people. Doing something well is what so many people dream about. What they do not dream is that it took hard work to get there. They have fallen in love with the glamour of success, but they do not want to put in the enormous amounts of time, concentrated effort, and hard work to attain it. Some people would not lift a finger to physical labor, but they will demand any amount of heavy work by tongue, when someone else is doing the lifting. Men who have labored hard in a quiet way to satisfy their craving for individual independence, have gained through hardship something that is worthwhile, even if their hopes and dreams have yet to materialize.

The mastery of those thick vague spaces between babyhood, childhood, our career years, and old age distinguishes our views of daily life. Because people associate with like-minded friends and family, they come to think of their own beliefs as middle-of-the-road norm. After enough work days are completed, enough words read, enough places visited, and enough people met, our views become broadened.

At times, though I complained about the long hours and working everyday of the week, the newspaper delivery business has taught me valuable lessons and resiliency.

The memories remain.

"DANCING WITH BEES"

Colony collapse disorder is a disorder that has devastated the honeybee population nationwide. Since the turn of the twenty-first century, it has increasingly affected the European honeybee, which is the primary pollinator in United States agriculture. Scientists are concerned about the decline in the honeybee caused by a dramatic increase in attacks by parasitic mites and the greater use of pesticides and chemicals in recent years. A single-cell protozoan organism seems to be the main parasite infesting honeybees and causing a major collapse of many hives. Beekeepers are convinced pesticides are playing a role after finding chemicals, previously sprayed on crops, in the dead hives.

Honeybees are important pollinators of the nation's crops and vegetables. When honeybees visit flowers, pollen adheres to their bodies and when they travel from flower to flower, they transfer the pollen, thus pollinating each plant. Flowers adequately pollinated produce larger, better-shaped fruits, vegetables, or nuts, with better taste.

We must understand the important benefits of honeybee pollination. The work of beekeepers around the country helps ensure our nation's food supply. The average American may experience increased food prices and decreased food supply if honeybees continue to disappear at the current rate. Much of United States agriculture depends on honeybee pollinators, and scientists estimate that one out of every three bites of food we take relates directly or indirectly to this process.

On one unusual day in August of 2001, it would have been difficult to explain this honeybee collapse to me. Just days earlier, a maintenance contract was negotiated to have the parking lot swept at Bowling Lanes, Inc. Bowling Lanes is a clean and comfortable twenty-four-lane bowling center, complete with a full-service lounge and snack bar open during business hours. Offered at this establishment, everything from birthday parties, corporate meetings, and league bowling ensures fun for the entire family. The owners, retired professional bowlers, own the bowling-alley establishment, and Lots of Curb Appeal, LLC, providing the parking lot sweeping services to them, is owned by the Hubele family. On the first Sunday morning in August of 2001, normal early routine on Sunday is driving to the bowling alley in order to sweep the parking lot; the job normally takes about two hours to complete. The bowling-alley establishment is located on a heavily traveled county road, part of a small township in St. Louis County, Missouri. The township is approximately four miles from the city limits and just a few miles from the location and headquarters of my sweeping business.

On the southeast corner of the bowling-alley parking lot, dead barren tree limbs hang out all over the tops of the slats of the wooden white picket fence. A big green trash dumpster sits in the same area. After completing most of my sweeping duties, I parked the sweeping truck, a Tymco manufactured 210 model with an Isuzu style cab-over.

It is interesting to know that the same style sweeper truck used by my company is used halfway around the world by semimodernized tribesmen to clean up the remains of food scraps fed to hyenas in Ethiopia. Andrew Zimmern, host of *Bizarre Foods* on the Travel Channel, journeys to places like Ethiopia to eat raw meat, Singapore to eat fish eyeballs or cooked deer penis, and Barcelona to eat a salad covered with cold pigeon innards.

A favorite episode of *Bizarre Foods* shows bush women holding sticks, branches, and a handmade, hollowed-out microphone imitating the body movements and idiosyncrasies of Andrew Zimmern, the boom operator and the cameraperson while working in Africa. The women had their walks down perfectly. As they spent more time together, the bond between the bush people and the film crew was an amazing event. Once during the taping, men of the bush scolded Andrew Zimmern for wanting to cut the string on a bird trap to retrieve a catch instead of untying it. The men of the bush reuse all of their supplies, not wasting a thing, because materials are not always plentiful in the bush. Americans can learn a lot from the people of the bush.

Another interesting story on the Travel Channel was about a man named Greg Car, who builds schools and hospitals in Africa. He is helping people become self-sustaining in the poorest regions of the world. His organization is protecting animals on the endangered list in areas designated as tourist destinations, creating jobs and raising money for the locals while educating them about poaching at the same time. Poachers have killed so many exotic big animals just to sell their body parts and tusks. Just like the bumper sticker reads, "Mean people suck." It applies to those poachers. Today, there are seven hundred gorillas in Congo and eight hundred elephants left in Africa, eight hundred polar bears left in Alaska and less than a thousand humpback whales left in ocean waters. Everything big in the animal kingdom seems to be vanishing, just as the dinosaurs became extinct hundreds of thousands of years ago.

There are only a few groups of people left still working the ancient ways of the mahouts. Mahouts are young men who stay with a newborn elephant for his entire life. They train, feed, and live with an elephant as a person stays with a pet such as a dog or cat in this country. Elephants live an average of seventy years, and just their enormous size easily conjures up thoughts of some of the difficulties a mahout might experience, especially getting chased by a mad or sick animal. Authorities hope that these courageous and disciplined people will continue their work and get the help they need in the future.

Let us get back to the parking lot. After stepping out of the truck to throw a bucketful of trash into the dumpster—trash that I handpicked off the grassy landscaped islands—and walking back toward the truck, suddenly out of nowhere, these honeybees started attacking me.

Here I was running around in the middle of this empty parking lot at 3:00 a.m. on a Sunday morning. I was trying to get away from the area of the honeybees, but apparently, I ran right toward the tree that nestled the bees' hive. All I could see was a large black swarm of honeybees buzzing around my head and upper body.

If astronauts can survive six months living at the international space station exposed to the elements, high amounts of radiation, bone density loss, weightlessness, low oxygen levels, loss of cabin pressure, and many other dangers, certainly this sweeper truck person can deal with a swarm of irritating bees flying around in the air. Anyone alive on July 20, 1969, remembers the statement by Neil Armstrong during his historic walk on the moon when he said, "One small step for man, one giant step for mankind." Many giant steps became the focus on this bowling-alley parking lot, just a small speck of this whole microcosm.

With hopes of outrunning the bees, I abruptly changed direction and ran faster toward the other side of the parking lot. Suddenly, I felt the first sting, then the next, then another, and so on and so forth. A brief question or two ran through my mind: "Does anyone else see what is happening? Can anyone help me get away from these honeybees?" To answer my own questions, "No, of course, it is three in the morning and most people are sleeping." I kept running, jumping, kicking, waving my arms dancing, and making moves I did not even know I was capable of doing. After sprinting around for thirty seconds or so—it seemed more like three hours—I tripped on a fallen branch and fell to the ground. I had been stung so many times; I just barely had my wits about me. However, I finally was able to make it back inside the truck, fighting off and killing a few honeybee stragglers clinging to my body, and safely drive four miles to return home; the memory of doing that is vague and dizzying.

Vertigo is one of the most common health problems in adults. According to the National Institutes of Health, about four of ten people in the United States experience prolonged feelings of dizziness at least once during their lifetime. Prevalence is slightly higher in women and increases with age.

Many sweeping truck drivers and taxi drivers experience vertigo because of all the left and right turns involved while trying to perform their jobs. Vertigo refers to the sensation of dizziness or spinning that occurs because of a disturbance in balance. Running around trying to get away from swarms of bees can bring about these symptoms. Lightheadedness and unsteadiness occur because of a disorder in the vestibular system, the structures of the inner ear, the vestibular nerve, brainstem, and cerebellum. The vestibular system is responsible for sight and movement and for keeping objects in focus as the body moves. Vertigo is an uncomfortable health problem all by itself, but when combined with attacking stinging bees, the symptoms are even worse.

Once arriving at home, my daughter, Allison, applied an appropriate insect-bite ointment and alternating warm and cold compresses to my forehead, administered acetaminophen for pain while simultaneously pulling out at least fifty stingers out of my skin. For the next four or five hours, I slept. When I awoke, my swollen face and head felt like it was the size of a watermelon on steroids. The next day, things slowly got better, but there were remnants of the experience, as evidenced by itching rashes, red spots, and countless welts on all of my extremities.

My whole body felt like it was recovering from some kind of reaction to a food allergy. "According to the Centers for Disease Control and Prevention, more than 3 million American children and teenagers have food or digestive allergies, which commonly include sensitivity to milk, peanuts, eggs, wheat, soy, shellfish and fish." [5]

Outnumbered and battling so many honeybees firsthand, I wondered, "How could there be a honeybee disorder?" I concluded that either way, too many honeybees or a shortage of honeybees, both are problems.

This dancing-with-bees experience at Bowling Lanes, the tenth customer when we started our parking lot sweeping company, did not deter us from growing the business. Within five years after starting the business, the company was servicing over three hundred parking lots per month. In the summer of 1996, a reporter for the *St. Louis Post-Dispatch* newspaper wrote the following about our company, with a photograph of a sweeping truck appearing above the article titled "The Man, the Truck, the Moment: Parking Lot Business is Taking Off."

Steve Hubele, president of Lots of Curb Appeal, stood showing off the trucks that are the bases of his parking lot cleaning company.

"It's a toy," he said with a grin as he pointed out the hula-hoop-size brushes that rotate and sweep dust and debris into the pickup head, which looks and functions as a big vacuum and deposits trash into the hopper. The hopper resembles the container on a trash truck and dumps the waste into a recycling bin. What a plethora of switches and engines, two to be precise, and gears for a man to play with.

With three of these marvels, Hubele and his four employees sweep three hundred parking lots a month. He charges fifty dollars on average to clean a lot. He is able to pay himself a salary of $50,000 a year, and the business is growing.

Hubele, whose home and business are in south St. Louis County, is a steady sort who speaks with deliberation. Nevertheless, when he talks about cleaning parking lots, he becomes a bit animated. It is an odd little niche business. He says he has three serious competitors in the bi-state area. The industry began in the past ten years, since the number of strip malls and shopping centers increased and the trucks became available.

Hubele was a teacher, a salesperson, and a newspaper carrier. He has a master's degree in technology from Webster University. He always wanted to work for himself and make his own business decisions. He says Lots of Curb Appeal uses many of the skills he picked up over the years from sales and planning to customer service and computer skills. He designed his brochure on a computer.

The brochure outlines every reason imaginable for getting a parking lot cleaned. Some such as, "A clean environment has proven to increase profits, stands to reason." Others bring brand new images of neglected parking lots to mind, "Unswept parking areas attract pests, rodents, disease-carrying animals."

Ten years ago, in addition to delivering the Post-Dispatch, Hubele cleaned a few businesses inside and out. It was then he saw the trucks that could make some aspects of his tasks so much simpler.

He found the trucks on the Internet and in 2001, he bought the first one for $40,000. He sold a few people on the service before he put the money down.

Lots of Curb Appeal cleans parking lots from 9 p.m. to 6 a.m., but Hubele does not mind the hours. He says he schedules one day a week off, and having daytime hours free means he is able to coach the softball teams of his two daughters, Amanda and Allison.

Trucks are not the only machines Lots of Curb Appeal uses. The company has backpack blowers, lawnmowers and weed whackers. Sometimes the employees pick up the debris by hand.

Steve Bruce, a manager at Norrenberns, a hardware store off Tesson Ferry Road, said of Hubele's service, "They do a great job. My people were trying to sweep it with a broom. Steve does so much more."

Hubele said hiring his company was less expensive, if you counted benefits, than getting an employee to do the work, and he thought businesses were beginning to realize that.

Surviving as a parking lot sweeper means keeping a thick skin, working hard, and sweeping up millions of tons of other people's messes (debris—garbage—G A R B O D G E is the French pronunciation—trash). This includes sweeping up used discarded diapers, roadkill, paper wrappers, cigarette butts, cardboard boxes, tin cans, plastic water bottles and plastic soda bottles, tons of beer bottles, glass liquor bottles, and used condoms thrown on parking lots. Sweeping so much trash of all kinds and so many leaves in the fall months that your body feels like an extension of a tree—any kind of tree. When sweeping after salt, spread to melt the ice and snow in the winter months, you work twice as hard because you have to cover every square inch of the parking lots. In the winter, in a rush to get out of the cold and into a warm car, people drop things in parking lots. Sometimes you get lucky and find dollar bills—fives, tens, and an occasional twenty—even winning scratch-off lottery tickets dropped by an unsuspecting customer of one of the business establishments that sells them. You can always find loose change near drive-up windows at fast food restaurants and banks.

Once I heard a caller telling a story on the channel-9 public broadcasting show *Donnybrook*, a talk show about national and local events filmed in studio in downtown St. Louis. This is absolutely one of the best talk shows in the country. The caller was complaining about some of the mishaps of the Missouri Department of Transportation (DOT) and the lack of communication within internal divisions. He explained how late one evening, he passed a highway street sweeping truck working the inner lane along the concrete median. Just a quarter of a mile further along on the highway, in front of the sweeper truck, a paint striping truck was re-marking the lines. Recounting the story of this blunder, he referred to the men in charge as, "Mo-DOT, Larry-DOT, and Curly-DOT." The sweeper truck did not belong to Lots of Curb Appeal, LLC.

Some nights operating the sweeper truck are routine, but other nights sometimes something happens to make that night unique. Like the night, I saw a black cougar lunge across Bowles Avenue and vanish into a residential neighborhood. An animal from the big cat family is unmistakable because of its size, girth, strength, and ability to pounce when it runs. It is very rare to see a misplaced black cougar in a metropolitan area of over two million people.

Working to clean a parking lot after a school picnic, I picked up a live copperhead snake, thinking it was one of many discarded rubber snakes given out as a table prizes.

Another night, after bending down to pick up a discarded paper cup on a grassy area adjacent to a skating rink parking lot, working in the rain and thick fog, I came face to face with an owl resting on top of a fence post. My big blue eyes spooked its big brown eyes, causing it to bellow a startled hoot and fly away while I just stood there, my heart racing a little faster.

A landscape company does the mowing, planting, trimming bushes, weeding, and mulching at a Midwest Banking Center in Fenton, Missouri. After they finish their work, our company swept the parking lot and drive-through areas in order to clean up the grass clippings, mulch, trash, and debris. Earlier in the morning of this particular day, the landscaping crew spread new pine bark mulch around the bushes and on the landscaped grassy areas. The landscapers inadvertently completely covered up a loose manhole lid with pine bark mulch. During the late evening of this same day, while walking on a newly mulched grassy area to pick up trash, I suddenly fell in a manhole. Not aware of or seeing the mulch covered loose sewer lid, I fell about five feet down into this manhole. Luckily, I was able to grab onto the top surrounding concrete edges, avoiding a full twelve-foot descent to the bottom of the sewer. The fall caused scrapes on the backs of my thighs and calves, but no serious injuries. After telling this manhole story to my sister Kathy over a telephone conversation, she said, "Thank goodness you caught yourself. I can picture you down in a manhole for days, screaming, with no one coming to your rescue, like stories you see on the news."

Yet on another night, moments after crossing the bridge over the Missouri River going east on Interstate 70, I watched some crazy person driving a rusted green late Oldsmobile, going at least eighty miles per hour, pass my vehicle almost as if standing still. It is not out of the ordinary to see people driving too fast or speeding almost every night. However, the crazy person driving the rusted green Oldsmobile was going at least eighty miles per hour with no back wheels. The rear axle dragging on the pavement at such a high speed produced sparks forming the appearance of a giant fireball traveling down the highway, a Walmart store seen in the distant darkness of the night.

Walmart has more stores in America than any other retailer. Their customers want to save money and still buy great products from a large choice of assortments. "Our greatest opportunities are still ahead of us," according to Michael Duke, their president and CEO, on a television interview. Though there are several Walmart stores in the St. Louis metropolitan area, Lots of Curb Appeal, LLC has not been able to secure a contract to sweep any of their parking lots. For whatever reason, mainly not able to offer the lowest price and still make a profit, negotiations have not produced any additional work for our company.

The process of sales talks and negotiations in hopes of securing more business is not always a complete success, but it is never squandered or wasted. Walmart taught me how they are trying to use renewable energy, reduce waste, and put more environmentally friendly products on the shelves at the stores. They are buying new delivery trucks with more efficient gas mileage to replace their outdated fleets. All of their stores use energy-efficient electric light bulbs to be more environmentally responsible and cut down costs. In addition, bananas are the number one food item sold in their stores around the world; at a price that they make sure is the lowest.

The memories remain.

Because there are fewer people out, less traffic, and fewer distractions when working nights, a person is more aware of things not noticed during the hustle and bustle of the daytime. Some things only occur at night.

At night, the sky is full of interesting things such as the stars, the Big Dipper, the Little Dipper, the light of the moon, and the different shapes of the clouds. Some things that happen at night are just strange.

The sweeping truck rolled into the mostly vacant west parking lot at Kutis Funeral Home on Gravois Road in the late evening of a September 2008 night. In the middle of the parking lot sat a white, rectangular-shaped, portable cooler device. Human organs harvested for transplants typically are stored in such devices, with ice or a perfusion bath to keep it healthy longer. Lifeport Transporters delivers hearts, livers, kidneys, and pancreases locally and regionally, and Airnet's specialty carriers make coast-to-coast transports. Airnet ships a number of medical items, including organs, blood products, tissue specimens, and implant devices. Operating rooms around the country carefully remove organs during evening hours because hospitals are less busy at night. Specialty aircraft transport over four hundred organs to more than one hundred major cities every weeknight.

Thoughts raced through my mind thinking about this white cooler device, out of place all by itself in the middle of the parking lot. As the sun was about to set, I thought it was probably very important to notify a medical professional; a decision to look at the contents inside the cooler device cleared my vision. After unlocking the two fastening clamps and lifting back the top lid, the smell was almost unbearable and after quickly glancing at some kind of bloody fleshy part inside the cooler device, the lid immediately dropped back into place. Because this organ did not ship to proper destination on time, did some unfortunate person die?

Never before dealing with a biomedical company engaged in commercial portable hypothermia-oxygenated preservation and transport technology of human organs, it was time to make another decision, a decision to look again inside the cooler device.

This time, after raising the lid, you could see an eyeball floating on top of the contents inside the container. The smell seemed even worse this time. Further observation of the contents made everything much clearer: the portable cooler device contained a portion of discarded fish parts. Apparently, after a successful fishing trip, the portable cooler device must have been stored in the back of the car, but forgotten about for several days. Discovering that the container remained in the car, the smell inside the car became so bad that the driver or the driver's wife insisted on dumping it right where the car parked in the middle of the funeral home parking lot. Too much to bear, someone else would deal with it later.

The memories remain.

Seaman George Walter Hubele Jr., enlisted in the United States Navy and stationed at Pearl Harbor in 1948.

George Walter Hubele Jr. and Audrey Margaret Juengst on their wedding day, April 18, 1953.

Steve hitting an iron shot during a golf outing in earlier days.

We even found a baseball game to watch in Anchorage, Alaska where they play a short seven week season.

Photograph of Allison having some fun at the "Go Kiss a Moose" cutout in Talkeetna, Alaska.

Photograph of Allison taking a break at the Beluga Whale Rest-stop north of Anchorage, Alaska.

Photograph of white birds called "kittywicks" circling mountain range and waterfall in Prince William Sound.

Photograph of Steve and daughter Allison onboard cruise ship in Prince William Sound near Whittier, Alaska.

Photograph of Allison and the friend she found while visiting Talkeetna, Alaska.

Photograph of moose crossing on Denali Highway north of Wasilla, Alaska

Photograph of "old Salt Mine" near Girdwood, Alaska.
Dad always said, "Off to the Old Salt Mine",
when referring to leaving for work in the morning.

Photograph of Amanda graduating with a Master's Degree
from Webster University in St. Louis, MO.

Photograph of U.S.S. Arizona Memorial at Pearl Harbor, Oahu, Hawaii.

Photograph of Amanda and Allison at the Pearl Harbor Memorial Site, Oahu, Hawaii.

Photograph taken by Allison during visit to U.S.S. Arizona Memorial, looking up towards American Flag and God-like image of cloud.

Photograph of the St. Louis Arch.

The landmark known as Ronnies Drive-In since 1948, closed in 1983 and was bulldozed to the ground.

New Busch Stadium is the home of the St. Louis Cardinals baseball team.

"BAD MEALS"

Casa Botín restaurant in Central Spain, located on Cutler's Street in the heart of Madrid's old commercial center, is one of the best restaurants in the world. Ernest Hemingway made the restaurant famous and *Guinness Book of Records* proclaimed Casa Botín (founded in 1725) the world's oldest restaurant. Ancient archways, descending stone steps illuminated by old wrought-iron lanterns, patched crumbling walls and the brick-lined dining room are all part of its history.

Casa Botín is famous for serving one-month-old, seven—pound whole suckling pigs cooked in an eighteenth-century woodstove fueled by sweet smelling green oak logs. The main course might include rice, beans cooked in a special sauce, fried bread, and other dishes using secret ingredients.

The thing about food ingredients is that they are often only as good as the cook's ability to use them correctly in a recipe. Throw together some olive oil, small chunks of beef, dried beans, broccoli spears, salt, and a couple of other things and you can make a delicious bowl of stir-fry. However, add some mustard to the recipe or too much salt and you will turn something tasty into something nasty.

On the night of August 7, 2009, my dish of stir-fry and rice turned out wonderful—so wonderful, I ate two bowls full. To help digest my food, I decided to sit in my favorite brown leather chair and read a book. I enjoy reading books about cross-country travel in America. About one-third the way into my book, the author, Robert Sullivan, was explaining about the early days of travel in America.

The wagons leaving St. Louis during the westward movement of the 1840's were loaded up with beef, rice, dried beans, vinegar, flour, coffee, salt, and sugar (some of the same stir-fry food ingredients I had just finished eating). They headed out from St. Louis, overland travelers following rivers such as the Missouri or the Platte, staying close to water for bathing, cooking, or drinking. Women cooked in wind and rain, and when they could not find firewood, they used buffalo manure to start a fire. Buffalo were abundant in those days. The manure burned clean and with little scent. [6]

Today's chefs use many of the same food ingredients used by the early westward travelers. Spoiled with modern conveniences and appliances, just the thought of using buffalo chips as fuel to cook and drinking water straight out of today's polluted rivers would turn a good meal into a bad meal.

On many Saturday mornings, during many of our childhood years of the late fifties, Dad would fix breakfast for my sisters and me. Preparation was a lengthy affair that could last up to two hours to get everything just right. His specialty (the only meal he ever made us for breakfast . . . Mom made all the others) he called, "jelly bread egg sausage sandwiches served on a toasted bun." This was several years before McDonald's opened its first store in St. Louis—actually Crestwood—Missouri, about a three-mile drive from our house. A few years later, McDonald's expanded with stores at several other locations in the St. Louis area and began offering a very familiar morning sandwich called the Breakfast Mac. This breakfast sandwich was eerily similar to the same sandwich Dad had been making us for more than ten years. When thinking about the possibilities of how to prepare food, Dad was definitely ahead of his time. All the breakfast sandwiches Dad prepared tasted great and his meticulous time-consuming efforts were much appreciated, but after McDonald's started serving them, Dad's were considered bad meals because our family never realized any financial rewards from them.

The fast-food giant, the burden of the beast, upstaged Dad without him even knowing what a great idea he had. I take that back—we had Dad and he had us, all to ourselves in our own kitchen for two solid hours every Saturday; we were not upstaged.

The memories remain.

One day in early fall of 1989, I was sitting on the sofa watching television. The voice of the channel five local news anchors was blaring across the room as my daughter Amanda, five years old at the time stood waiting by the living room window, staring out toward the street in front of our house. This was her daily routine. She would lean on the windowsill anticipating seeing her mother pull up in the driveway, returning home after an eighteen-mile trip in traffic from the office where she worked. Wife Kimberly (Amanda and Allison's mom) worked as a data processor and inside salesperson for a privately owned successful process controls distributorship called BDC, Inc—the owners' names are Ben, Don, and Charlie.

On this particular weekday night in October, a cool and breezy fall evening, we planned a special dinner of liver and onions. Liver is high in proteins and iron. As a rule of thumb, it is advisable to eat your ideal target weight in grams of protein per day. If a man's target weight is 180 pounds, he can eat 180 grams of protein per day. Some people do not like liver and onions, but since I did, Kimberly prepared it for me a few times per year. The frozen meat previously thawed for most of the afternoon, and the raw onions were sitting out on the kitchen counter.

On this night, as any other given work night, at the usual time of 5:45 p.m., Kimberly arrived home from work. Once she spotted the car driving down our street and excited to see her mother, Amanda ran from the windowsill to the front door to joyfully hug her mom and talk about the day's events at kindergarten. After going through a hectic day at the office and engaging the maze of traffic on the way home, mother joined daughter in changing in to comfortable clothes, usually a T-shirt and baggy jeans.

After settling in to the satisfying surroundings of home, Kimberly decided to do a load of laundry. She filled the yellow measuring cup with detergent and she transferred the dirty clothes from the hamper basket into the washing machine. Before she could finish what she was doing, the wall telephone rang. Not paying much attention to the minor interruption, with the measuring cup still in hand, she raced up the basement steps to answer the phone. She set the yellow measuring cup of detergent on the laminated kitchen counter and focused her attention on the telephone conversation with her close neighbor friend named Peggy. In the middle of her conversation with Peggy, Kimberly decided to preheat the frying pan and fill another yellow measuring cup with flour to use for gravy because she was about to start cooking the liver and onions. A few minutes later, after finishing her informal talk with Peggy, Kimberly placed the thawed liver into the frying pan and the sizzling noise seemed to indicate that the oil temperature was just right for cooking. Next, she reached for the yellow measuring cup and proceeded to spread the ingredients over the liver and onions. It was only a matter of time before we would be enjoying our special meal.

Kimberly decided to put another load of laundry into the washing machine and then she joined Amanda and me, as all three of us retired to the living room sofa to relax for a while as our meal cooked. We occasionally enjoyed watching reruns of *The Cosby Show*, and tonight was no different. (Tonight's episode focused on how to discipline kids and after being told several times to tidy her room, Rudy was in trouble for not doing so.) About halfway through the show, I happened to glance over toward the kitchen. To my astonishment, hundreds of tiny air bubbles were circulating around in the air and escaping into other rooms in the house.

It did not take long for Kimberly to realize her mistake. Obviously, she had poured the yellow measuring cup full of white detergent on to the liver, and the yellow measuring cup full of flour into the washing machine. Would the liver taste like soap and would our clothes smell like bread? With hopes of salvaging our meal, Kimberly rinsed off the liver and cooked it again in flour. The thought of overcooked liver reminded me of a study done by Japanese researchers that suggested a link between overdone meat and cancer. In an attempt to show appreciation for her effort, agreeing to taste just one bite, it was painfully evident that this meal would have to be a do-over on another day. In addition, after working through several more wash cycles, but using detergent this time, our clothes got clean and they even smelled good.

The memories remain.

My day started watching Matt Lauer on the *Today Morning Show*. He talked about the Kentucky Derby and picked Smarty Jones to continue his unbeaten streak by predicting him to win the Preakness, the second leg of the triple crown. Matt stated, "My fellow employees and I only bet cookies in the office pool." After finishing my morning cup of coffee, I turned off the television set. It was time to head out the front door because yesterday, I promised Dad I would help him pick out a new lawnmower. Dad's fifteen-year-old Walmart special went kaput.

Dad and I jumped in the car and took the fifteen-minute drive to Home Depot to pick out the best selection to fit our needs. Home Depot advertises that they have experienced, knowledgeable, and courteous factory-trained service technicians. Home Depot usually has very competitive prices and the technician helping us on this day appeared very professional while providing us with onsite product demonstrations. Nevertheless, no matter what our sales technician said or showed us, my seventy-three-year-old father knew exactly what he wanted to buy. Dad did not want a more expensive self-propelled lawnmower, bag grass-catcher, fancy wheels, electric start, or anything bigger or heavier. He wanted the same basic lawnmower he used for the past fifteen years because he was comfortable working it and it lasted fifteen years without any mechanical breakdowns. Therefore, when Dad finally saw this lawnmower, the same basic model as the one he bought fifteen years ago, sitting at the end of the aisle in the corner of the showroom floor, he enthusiastically said, "I will take that one." This lawnmower had a Briggs and Stratton engine; it was lightweight and easy to push. Because it did not have all the extra bells and whistles, it only cost 139 dollars. Next, we paid the cashier, loaded the lawnmower into the back of my Chevrolet Tahoe, and headed for home.

As we pulled into the driveway, Dad and I saw Mom sitting on the front porch. She was not a bit surprised to see that we bought a new lawnmower identical to the old model. All the colors of this supposedly new lawnmower stayed the same over time; the only difference is now some of the parts are plastic-injection molds instead of fabricated steel. Mom watched as we assembled the handle, added oil and gasoline to the tank, and rolled the lawnmower into the storage shed located in the far corner of the backyard. The yard needed mowing, but the grass was still very wet from three days of almost continuous rainy weather, causing a delay of outside work until the next day.

The three of us went back inside the house for lunch.

Mom prepared our lunch. Each of our plates consisted of two tuna sandwiches on found French rolls, two large green olives, and a short stack of Lay's potato chips. Each of us drank a tall glass of lemon-flavored iced tea on the rocks to help wash down our food.

Moments after finishing lunch, we decided to play Scrabble, mainly because we felt lazy after eating and listening to the heavy downpour hit the roof. Since I worked nights sweeping parking lots and Mom and Dad were retired, this turned out to be a good call, a nice way to spend some quality time together. Mom was an avid reader of all types of books, and Dad was a crossword-puzzle player for the past fifty years, a hobby he started during his navy days carrying out extended missions on submarines in the late 1940s during the Korean War years. I was just hoping to hold my own against this stiff competition.

Mom won the first game uncontested. I started the second game by spelling the word "scorer." Dad was our official game scorer and he recorded ten points for me on this initial play. Playing Scrabble, Mom and Dad always showed a keen sense for maximizing their opportunities by using the double-letter and triple-word squares whenever possible. Our game continued; we took turns picking letters and placing words strategically on the game board. Soon I felt like I gained an advantage over Mom and Dad, because the luck of the draw seemed to place in my hands, more of the letters with higher point values. However, with much experience studying the game and great strategic play by Mom and Dad, the score stood close:

Steve—145 points
Dad—137 points
Mom—137 points

By this stage, near the end of the game, all of the letters were gone from the grab bag. Each of us had three letters left to play. Mom was next to play her turn. She skillfully placed her last three letters at the end of the word "zoo," forming two new words, "zoom" horizontally and "mob" vertically. This maneuver earned Mom an additional thirty-six points to win the game. Though our agreement is the lowest scorer buys the highest scorer a bag of their favorite cookies, we really just play for fun. Before we could congratulate Mom for a game well played, she started laughing hysterically. She almost started choking from laughing so hard. Dad and I fixed her a tall glass of water. Finally, after several sips of water, a calming effect allowed mom to relax and get her breath.

Figuratively speaking, just as the mob went zoom in their fast cars, Mom quickly exclaimed in an underworldly fashion, "Didn't you two idiots realize that the letter *m* that I used to form the words 'mob' and 'zoom' was not really the letter *m*?" She went on to explain, "I did not have a play with the letter *w*, and so, by turning it upside down, the letter *w* appeared to be the letter *m*." After realizing Mom's mischievous maneuver, now, all three of us were laughing uncontrollably.

Just as I started my morning listening to Matt Lauer talking about making a bet and playing for cookies, the three of us spent the afternoon having fun, the result of making a bet and playing for cookies.

The memories remain.

Good food, good service, and clean surroundings keep successful restaurants in business. It is nice to enjoy a relaxing night with friends or family at a great restaurant, not having to prepare the food or clean up the mess. The servers rush back and forth and everywhere you look, people are shoveling food into their mouths as if it might be the last meal they eat. Sometimes the food is fantastic. Waiters bring out anything from great cuts of thick juicy steaks, superb platters of seafood, and mountains of buttery mashed potatoes to homemade rolls, house-specialty soups, and freshly tossed salads. However, sometimes you just do not have time to go eat a meal at a restaurant, so you settle for a snack at home. On this day, I was settling for a snack.

Off the pantry shelf, I grabbed the Easy Cheese in an air-pressurized aluminum can to have an easy snack. This pressurized processed American cheese spread was made with real cheese; I just was not sure where the cheese processed in East Hanover, New Jersey came from. This product is also available in other flavors: cheddar, sharp cheddar (careful not to cut your mouth when chewing), cheddar bacon, and nacho. Maybe the bacon comes from New Jersey cows. Oh! Make a correction: bacon usually comes from the harvested meat of pigs and turkeys.

No need to refrigerate this product, but I found out the cheese smells bad if you leave it on a shelf and forgot about it for ten years. Easy Cheese is perfect for portable snacking, but the cheese tastes bad if, before eating it, you left it on a shelf and forgot about it for ten years. Low in sugar, high in protein and calcium, but does the body no good if, before eating it, you left it on a shelf and forgot about it for ten years.

Easy Cheese ingredients include non-cultured milk as opposed to cultured milk. Maybe this is why the cheese went bad: milk from a dumb cow. Ingredients include whey (who is on first, what is on second, why is on third); what is whey? Ingredients include *carrageen an annatto*. These extracts were starting to get to my head as I envisioned a beautiful Italian woman named Ann wishing to take a water-carriage ride in Venice with me.

The side of the can says, "For complaints or comments in writing to us, please enclose number from the bottom of the can (2216AY0632057) or call 1-800-622-4726 weekdays, 9:00 a.m.-7:30 p.m., EST." First, there is no address on the pressurized air aluminum can, unless the address is on the inside of the can, so I cannot write to them. Second, I am not going to call to complain, because I left this product on the shelf and forgot about it for ten years. It is not their fault the cheese went bad.

Sometimes you do not have time to eat a meal, so you settle for a bad snack.

Dierbergs, Schnucks, and Shop 'n Save are the three largest grocery chains competing for business in the St. Louis area. Shop 'n Save is the store of choice for many people who want a wide selection for a cheaper price if you are willing to bag your own groceries. On the hottest day of the summer of 2009, I found myself in line with a full shopping cart of food waiting at the checkout aisle. After a couple of hours of grocery shopping, a good dinner usually follows the evening of that same day of shopping for groceries.

Angelina, an attractive forty-five-year-old woman from the Philippines, started working when she was eight years old and moved to the United States when her father died of alcoholism. She is the fastest and friendliest of all the cashiers and her usual workstation is at checkout aisle seven.

When it was my turn to unload groceries on the conveyor belt counter, Angelina paused to help an elderly man in a wheelchair bag his groceries. Many senior citizens shopped on Thursdays because Thursdays are double-coupon days. This day was a Thursday and cashiers work extra hard on Thursdays. Without hesitating and failing to give it much thought, I broke out of the line and proceeded to grab items from the end of the counter to help speed up the process of bagging groceries for the elderly man in the wheelchair. That turned out to be a mistake.

"Hey, you son of a bitch," said the old man in the wheelchair. "Hey, somebody help me, this son of a bitch is stealing my groceries!" All the noise and commotion overheard by the store manager positioned a few aisles away, fixing an electronic cash register out-of-tape issue, soon caused his attention to be diverted to aisle seven.

As Angelina was trying to explain to the elderly man in the wheelchair ("That gentleman was only trying to help us . . ."), the store manager quickly understood the circumstances and hustled over to calm the situation. The elderly man, as red-faced as the rest of us, apologized and went on his way, driving his electronic wheelchair back to his car in a handicap space in the parking lot. The situation was now under control. Maybe next time I encounter the elderly man in the wheelchair, we will talk about baseball.

By the time I put my groceries away at my home, my energy level was much lower than on most other nights after shopping for groceries. It had been a long day and the night consisted of eating a couple of simple snacks before retiring early to bed. The good meal that usually followed a day of shopping for groceries did not happen on this night, the hottest night of the summer of 2009.

The memories remain.

"TRIPS TO ALASKA AND HAWAII"

A father has a special bond with his daughter. It doubles the joy and divides the grief. Taking a dream vacation with a daughter enhances this relationship even more. On the first Sunday of August, during the summer of 2004, Allison and I flew to Anchorage, Alaska for an eight-day extravagant vacation. Approximately half a million people live in Alaska, with three out of five of them living in Anchorage. Juneau, and Fairbanks; each has a population near thirty thousand. Many of the other small towns in Alaska have less than one thousand people. Alaska is one-fifth the size of the rest of the lower United States.

We flew over Mount McKinley at 11:00 p.m., a monumental experience on a clear night, seeing the effects of the sun still glistening on the mountains slanted at generously obtuse angles to the ground as we prepared to land at the airport in Anchorage. At an altitude of 20,300 feet, the mountains covered in glacier ice and snow, green and brown alpine tundra in the distance is just barely visible through the big white peaks and the sparse clouds in the sky. From an overhead position in the sky, the pristine view makes you feel like you are closer to heaven.

Once you step foot onto Alaskan soil, the diversity of the people and their customs unique to the state are immediately evident. Alaska, significantly inhabited with Russians, Eskimos, Inuit Indians, Canadians, Japanese people, and Americans, offers a wealth of learning opportunities at every venture. The names Mulchatna, Unalaska, Fairbanks, Kiska, Allakaket, Bristol Bay, Ketchikan, and Kotzebue are beautiful symbols to the people who work, play, and live in theses areas.

When we travel, it is fun for Allison and me to slide the guestroom card into the slot to open the door to the hotel room, to check on all of the special amenities, to see what is on television, to see if they have a coffeepot and a hairdryer, and to see the view from the window. As we walked from the lobby, up the elevator to the third floor and down the long hall, the walls spoke volumes with photos of wildlife and landscapes native to Alaska. As we approached the entrance to our room, a man in his seventies was working to open the door with his magnetized plastic card. He swiped the card multiple times through the bronze-plated locking mechanism without any luck entering our room. When we confronted the elderly man, he realized his room was directly above ours on the fourth floor, as he had exited the elevator one floor early.

Our accommodations included a complimentary buffet with many choices and great coffee served around the clock. Every morning during our stay, my daughter Allison accompanied me to the breakfast nook, the best part of the complimentary buffet.

The view from our third-floor room at the Millennium Hotel was spectacular. Mountains, ocean waters, a seaplane water airport, and a fifty-thousand-acre military base surrounded Anchorage. Every few minutes, a seaplane lands on the water, visible from many of the rooms at the hotel, bringing back passengers from sightseeing tours and fishing trips, or transporting people doing business in Alaska. The mountains are essentially a full stop to Anchorage and this town has nowhere else to go.

For years, according to many of the locals in Anchorage, the talk has been to move the capital of Alaska to a more centrally located site near Anchorage or Fairbanks. The move would be very expensive for the taxpayers of the state and very damaging to the economy in Juneau. The legislators and politicians do not want to be close to the people because it is much easier to give lip service from a distance.

The concierge at our hotel, the Millennium Hotel of Anchorage, gave us a quick history lesson on the capital. Richard Harris founded Juneau as a mining district and wanted to name the town Harrisburg; however, in a dispute over other land claims, the courts deprived Harris of all his property and belongings. Harris eventually died in a sanatorium in Oregon. The land deeds transferred to Joe Juneau. In 1900, the year after Richard Harris died; the town became the capital of Alaska. Shady dealings have been part of politics from the beginning. Environmental land concerns, oil spills, state revenues, and education monies still evoke heated discussions and controversy today.

Because the federal government sold off land in lots at an auction in the 1950s, Eskimos lost the property they had communally owned for ten thousand years. Doctors, lawyers, engineers, and rich real-estate tycoons bought up most of the land. Sometimes it helps to have a little money in order to make a lot of money.

Because native Eskimos fought for preservation of lands and wildlife, combined with pressure to get the oil pipeline built, their claims yielded land settlements for Alaskan natives in 1971. The native Eskimos settled for forty million acres of land. Much of the land contains gold, silver, jade, and oil.

Everyone we met—citizens, concierges, hotel clerks, store clerks, government workers, cab drivers, shuttle bus drivers, waiters, and waitresses—was anxious to talk about the past or present and the evolution of Alaska, where it came from and where it is headed, mainly because tourism is their business and partly because it is so interesting.

When you travel, you learn things, gain new perspectives and reshape personal opinions. If you like to talk and you feel comfortable talking to complete strangers, you learn even more. Some Alaskans freely tell you that they receive four hundred dollars per person per year as a tax supplement paid for by state-earned big oil revenues. They tell you there is no shortage of oil and that big oil companies, the elite people of the world, and Middle Eastern rulers control the world. The elitists want the price of oil to reach one hundred fifty dollars per barrel. Prudhoe Bay has enough oil to supply America for several hundred years according to some scientists; the inner crusts of the earth replenish deep oil-drilling cavities anyway, they say. They tell you that Russia recently discovered oil at massive sites in the frozen tundra and they have the capability to drill forty thousand feet below the surface.

Our first day in Alaska, we decided to take a drive in our rented 2004 Chevrolet Caprice, along the Turn Again Arm of the Cook Inlet, a body of water extending off the Gulf of Alaska. I had to make an extra effort to concentrate on my driving; because at the same time, I thought about all the good times shared with my daughter Allison, the excitement of seeing this brilliant deep-blue ocean water and the prestigious and natural stage of the Chugach Mountains.

In the midst of the Alaskan summer, when the green grass grows tall and the leaves of the native trees glisten in the sunlight and much of the snow has melted, the panoramic view is spectacular. The tops of the mountains with scattered remnants of snow from the previous winter serving as eye candy and the warmth of the sun seems impossible that it is the end of summer. After driving for about an hour, I estimated our position in the car at sixty miles southeast of Anchorage; we were off the beaten path approaching the small town of Girdwood, with no people or buildings within our sight.

Several miles further down the road, we came upon an exit ramp and decided to pull off the highway. I drove a little farther down a secondary gravel road and soon noticed an old salt mine, which appeared vacant and inoperable for many years. I parked our rental car next to the rusted front entrance of the dilapidated metal building. The fresh smell of the tall green grass behind the building looked so inviting and the seventy-degree temperature was welcoming to two Midwesterners used to hot humid summers. When playing team sports back home, I always encouraged Allison to run fast. She enjoyed basketball, softball, and track during her youth. As soon as I stopped the car, Allison opened the passenger door and immediately ran past the old salt mine and toward the tall green native grasses. Abruptly, as if to disappear, she sank into the surface of the Alaskan earth. Seeming like overgrown wild grasses needing mowing, the vegetation actually was part of a type of northern arctic swampland, the end result of melted snow from glaciers from nearby Black Mountain. Luckily, she was able to catch her fall, but she still managed to paste herself in mud up to her knees. As I ran over to try to help, Allison was able to creep out of the wet sticky earth on her own. Mad and grossed out, she looked around and vented her frustration. She began to cry. I quickly went over to her, gave her a big hug, and tried to reassure her that she did not ruin her new tennis shoes, the ones she was wearing for the first time on this day.

Allison standing next to the road, partially covered in mud, looking cute to me, perfectly positioned in the reflective rays of the sunshine, I took her picture. "Allison, congratulations honey!" I said as gently as the situation allowed. She looked at me, embarrassed, confused, and still visibly upset.

"Why do you say that, Dad?" she asked.

I replied, "Well, now that you felt the burden of the swamp, you have to admit, this event will become funnier every time we tell the story."

"Yes, I guess you are right," she said. Her tears stopped. As we walked back to the car, she started to walk taller and I even heard her giggle.

On our second day in Alaska, we decided to drive our rented car to the town of Talkeetna. It is a two-hour drive to this quaint village, ninety-five miles north of Anchorage. From the center of town, the majestic skyline of Mount McKinley forms a postcard backdrop of an endless bright bluish sky, fog surrounding the highest elevations and a mountain clearing away everything lurking in the distance. Restaurants, coffeehouses, shops, bead factories, souvenir stands, and even two gas stations line Main Street. The television series *Northern Exposure* was filmed on location here. During the growing season, flowers and crops do well here. You can grow peas, potatoes, carrots, beets, cauliflower, broccoli, and many other vegetables in the south-central part of the state. Strawberries are particularly sweet and delicious, extra sweet due to the sugar buildup caused by six months of cool air and the long days of northern light during the growing season.

On our third day of enjoying this glorious frontier, we took a ride on the Alaskan Railroad. Our early morning journey took us from Anchorage to Whittier, a port town off the coast of Prince William Sound. We wanted to see something with no civilization in it, miles and miles of nothing but scenery. When you come from a big city, you get tired waiting in lines, driving in traffic, and paying taxes for things you do not believe in or do not know where the money is spent. However, I have always maintained that paying taxes for educational purposes is honorable, as long as the money provides for the intended purposes. The fresh air and the panorama helped us relax and forget about annoyances of the big city.

When you see some of the uninhabited landscapes that Alaska has to offer, you can feel what gives you energy. The wide-open space, fresh air, and the powerful stimulation to the senses gives this untapped land remarkable vigor.

Once we arrived in Whittier, about a four-hour train ride from Anchorage, we boarded a small cruise ship and took an eight-hour excursion along the shores of Prince William Sound and Black Mountain

Glacier. Surprises abound near almost every turn, as we saw porpoises, humpback whales, sea otters, bald eagles, calving glaciers, and kitty wicks. Kitty wicks are small white birds that lay their eggs during the later part of the summer. Literally thousands of kitty wicks assemble a verse of poetry along the cliffs, waterfalls streaming down from the glaciers. They take turns gracefully flying around in tight circles, seeming to be content on staying in one area of the mountain.

The Chugach Mountains are the northernmost of several mountain ranges up the coastal regions of the western edge of North America. The entire Chugach range is about five hundred kilometers (three hundred miles) long, partially running alongside the Glenn Highway and generally in an east-west direction. The breathtaking views can be attributed to its position along the Gulf of Alaska and the fact that there is more snowfall here than anywhere else in the world, an annual average of six hundred inches. The World Extreme Skiing Championships take place annually on the eastern slopes near the town of Valdez.

On the train ride back to Anchorage, we passed through tunnels that provide for railroad and automobile access through the mountains. We saw numerous full-horned Dall sheep high above the treetops, standing on the sides of cliffs, posing for passersby. For good visibility to heighten their awareness of predators, they migrate to the top spots in the mountain ranges of the Chugach Mountains of southern Alaska.

It is easy to conclude, as a train passenger enjoying the spectacular panoramic views, that the mountains are a popular destination for other outdoor activities, such as camping and salmon-fishing. Locals fish in the countless numbers of mountain streams and only keep their limit, abiding by Alaskan enhancement laws.

Typically, salmon are born in fresh water; migrate to the ocean, then return to fresh water to reproduce. Many salmon return to the exact spot they were born to spawn, but some crossover to populate new streams, such as those that emerge from melting of glacier ice. The concierge aboard our train explained, "In all species of Pacific salmon, the mature fish die within a few days of spawning, a trait known as semelparity. However, though not as common, some salmon survive and may spawn again, a trait known as iteroparity." Salmon has long been a big part of the Alaskan culture. Due to commercial net-fishing in other parts of the world, salmon population levels are a concern, however, Alaska stocks are still abundant.

On the fourth day of our trip, back in Anchorage, we dined in an atmosphere of warm Alaskan hospitality. The Sourdough Mining Company Restaurant is a replica of an old mill house. The menu offers a variety of selections: fresh Alaskan seafood, barbecued baby back ribs, salads, corn on the cob, baked beans, sandwiches, and their famous "Corn Fritters" with whipped honey butter. Broiled salmon and halibut are the best-selling items on the menu. You can enjoy refreshments from the full-service deck, while viewing Alaskan salmon in the backyard creek. Most patrons, including Allison and me, celebrated dessert by building our own ice cream sundae from an array of tasty toppings. This restaurant offers a complete dining experience in an early Anchorage townsite setting, with all the trimmings. After dinner, Dusty Sourdough and Miss Aura Lee, the owners, take you back to the gold rush days with song, storytelling, gold pan demonstrations, and lots of humor. For a delicious dinner in a warm and entertaining atmosphere of Alaskan hospitality, visit the Sourdough Mining Company Restaurant at 5200 Juneau Street in Anchorage, Alaska. Visitors from around the world visit this eating establishment.

On our fifth day in Alaska, we visited the Iditarod Trail Race Headquarters in Wasilla. This sled dog race called the "Greatest Race on Earth" takes place once per year. You cannot compare it to any other competitive event in the world. A race over 1,150 miles of the roughest, most beautiful scenery in the world, with jagged mountain ranges, frozen rivers, desolate tundra, and miles of windswept coast, throws many challenges at the mushers and their dog teams. Add to that temperatures fifty below zero, complete loss of visibility due to high winds blowing snow, long hours of darkness, and steep climbs, and you have the Iditarod. From Anchorage, in south-central Alaska, to Nome on the western Bering Sea coast, each team of twelve to sixteen dogs and their musher cover the distance in ten to seventeen days.

The Iditarod has won worldwide acclaim and interest. Japanese, German, Spanish, British, Russian, and American film crews have covered the event, as well as journalists from many major newspapers and magazines. The race, run by thousands of volunteers, take care of dog food, supplies, first-aid kits, and whatever is needed to help support the mushers at various checkpoints along the way.

According to information at the Iditarod National Historic Headquarters in Wasilla, the trail had its beginnings as a mail-and-supply route from the coastal towns of Seward and Knik to the interior mining camps at Flat, Ophir, Ruby, and beyond to the west coast communities of Unalakleet, Golovin, White Mountain, and Nome. Mail and supplies went in and gold was brought out via the dog sled. In 1925, part of the Iditarod Trail became a lifesaving highway for an epidemic that hit the town of Nome. Diphtheria threatened the lives of the people and serum had to arrive in town fast, during extreme weather conditions. Newspapers in New York City, Chicago, and around the nation followed the story as the mushers and their hard-driven dogs were able to accomplish the mission of saving hundreds of lives.

The Iditarod is a way for Alaskans to commemorate the past and honor their heroes. The route includes the large metropolitan area of Anchorage and goes through many small native villages along the way. Much activity and excitement takes place in areas that are otherwise quiet during the long months of Alaskan winter. The race is an educational opportunity for the young and an economic incentive for the old timers who relive the colorful Alaskan past.

On this day, daughter Allison and I met Joe Redington Jr., son of Joe Redington Sr., cofounder of the classic and affectionately known as the "Father of the Iditarod." Inside the Wasilla headquarters, Joe Jr. showed us certain pieces of equipment each team must have: an arctic parka, a heavy sleeping bag, an ax, snowshoes, people food, dog food, and boots for the dogs to protect against the cold and sharp ice injuries. Joe Jr. gave us a tour around the back of the building to see the kennels, a special breeding ground to raise future Iditarod puppies. At the kennels, Joe Jr. accidentally stepped on the foot of one of the puppies. The puppy continuously yelped louder than any full-grown breed of dog I had ever heard in my life. After a quick call by Joe on the cell phone, an assistant took the puppy away. Though the puppy received medical attention immediately, my daughter and I could not help but to wonder if the puppy had a broken foot.

Rick Swenson from Two River, Alaska is the only five-time winner of the race, never finishing out of the top ten. Libby Riddles became the first woman to win the Iditarod in 1985, though Susan Butcher became a four-time winner since that time. One of the most thrilling races happened in 1978 when Dick Mackey from Nenana, Alaska beat Rick Swenson by one second to achieve the impossible photo finish after two weeks on the trail.

The team that finishes in last place receives the "Red Lantern" trophy. Whether a team finishes first or last, they accomplish a feat that very few people even attempt, going the distance and establishing a place for their name in the Iditarod history books.

On the sixth and final day of our trip, we took a tour of the University of Alaska at Anchorage. All universities have a unique set of circumstances and obstacles to deal with in implementing their programs. Skyway walks, to shield people from the cold during the winter months, physically connect all of the buildings. Surprisingly, the University of Alaska and the Denali School District in Alaska, located in the Alaskan interior, near North America's tallest mountain, implemented one of the first one-to-one laptop programs. Each family is required to pay one hundred dollars to defray partial costs of the Internet service-provider network. Though Internet service is expensive in Alaska, the legislature approved long-time state funds, Alaska's Congress matched with federal funds and Apple helped with an outstanding lease plan. Alaska, under most unusual physical conditions, is able to maintain one of the best technology programs in the country. It pays off in educated students and tourism dollars.

While packing our belongings in our hotel room, watching the Discovery Channel, we learned about two polar bear cubs and their mother. The male cub learned to hunt and grew strong, but the female cub struggled, never learned to catch salmon or seals. Partly due to global warming and receding ice shelves, the female cub starved to death. It was difficult to watch this documentary; watching the cub become weak and frail, so thin that her ribs were sticking out through her fur coat.

Due to the difficulty of understanding death and talking about it with my youngest daughter for any extended length of time, the conversation changed but stayed on the same topic: bears. Allison made the comment, "Bears have feet just like humans, and not many animals have feet similar to humans." After giving that statement some thought, she is correct; most animals have either paws or hoofs. The only other quick response was that apes and animals that are members of the ape family have feet, though much hairier feet, resembling human feet.

Though our short summer stay gave us just a glimpse of all that Alaska has to offer, we learned the excitement and the dangers of this vast wide-open territory called Alaska. Though we visited Alaska during the short warm season, our conversations with others told us about the toughness of the longtime native residents and the brutality of the winter seasons. Everyone talked about the connection between big oil companies, carbon emissions, global warming, temperature of the ocean waters, and the disappearing ice shelves. It became increasingly evident that the lower forty-eight states has to do much more to become a greener planet so that people and animals can coexist. Recycling, reusing our natural resources, protecting our animals, and demanding that our politicians tell the truth and making our environment the top priority make a lot of sense. We enjoyed the spectacular scenery, but our favorite places were the places we shared with other people and animals. We had fun and learned about Alaska and its people—Alaskans tamed by the extreme winter weather conditions, wild animals, and rugged terrain.

The memories remain.

After a long ten-hour flight and a short taxi ride to our hotel, my daughters and I were standing in the open-air reception area of our new home for the next eight days. The first words you hear when arriving at the Hilton Hawaiian Village Beach Resort are "Aloha, welcome to our island paradise." Located on Waikiki's widest stretch of beach, the impressive vacation property is nestled on twenty-two prime acres, offering the perfect combination of luxury hotel accommodations and top-notch Hawaiian hospitality. The beach resort and spa show off their elegance with lush tropical gardens, lava rock waterfalls, exotic wildlife roaming the grounds, and priceless artworks throughout the four hotel towers and on the walls of the many restaurants on location.

The island of Oahu is a story of contrasts, from the majestic green vegetation growing on the cliffs of the Ko'olau Mountains in the middle of the island, to the enticing clear blue waters of the Pacific Ocean, or from the hustle and bustle of the beachgoers on Waikiki to the more reserved locals of North Beach. The island is a rewarding destination of natural beauty full of cultural events and historical sites.

Since both my daughters like to shop, Chinatown was one of the things on our to-do list while in the island of Oahu. The first Chinese immigrants started arriving in Oahu in 1852, and they began moving into an urban section of Honolulu and established a community, adding many small shops now known as Chinatown. Chinatown offers upscale Pacific Rim restaurants, open-air food markets, souvenir shops, noodle shops, and art galleries. We walked several miles and bought some souvenirs, a wooden totem pole statue, a few colorful plastic leis for the relatives back home, and some postcards. The girls bought purses.

The next day we visited Pearl Harbor. The three of us took the short ride across the bay in the Navy watercraft, a customized platoon boat to transfer tourists over to the *Arizona* Memorial. Every president of the United States since Franklin D. Roosevelt has made a pilgrimage to the site. The shrine at the far end is a marble wall that bears the names of all the men killed on the USS *Arizona*, enclosed behind maroon-colored velvet ropes.

The USS *Arizona* Memorial, located at Pearl Harbor, Honolulu, Hawaii, marks the resting place of 1,102 of the 1,177 sailors killed on the USS *Arizona* during the attack on Pearl Harbor on December 7, 1941, by Japanese imperial forces and commemorates the events of that day. The attack on Pearl Harbor and the island of Oahu was the action that led to the United States involvement in World War II. On that day, more than 2,400 Americans lost their lives in the harbor.

Today, the *Arizona* Memorial spans the hull of the sunken ship. Oil bubbles rising from the wreckage beneath the water still work their way to the surface of the water above nearly seventy years later. The oil seeping referred to by many as "the tears of the Arizona."

"Contrary to popular belief, the USS *Arizona* is no longer in commission. She is, however, an active United States military cemetery. As a special tribute to the ship and her lost crew, the United States flag flies from the flagpole, once attached to the severed mainmast of the sunken battleship. Now the flagpole attaches to the side of the memorial. The USS *Arizona* Memorial has come to commemorate all military personnel killed in the Pearl Harbor attack."

The structure of the memorial sags in the middle but rises up on the ends, symbolizing initial defeat and staying strong for an ultimate victory later. The overall effect of the design causes a feeling of serenity in the visitors. According to Honolulu architect Alfred Preis, "Overtones of sadness have been omitted to permit the individual to contemplate his own personal responses, his innermost feelings."

As we were standing reverently on deck, another customized watercraft carrying tourists sneaked up to the memorial from another direction, our sight partially blocked by the sun and other ships and vessels nearby.

Without much serious thought, someone among the group of tourists asked, "Where did that new group of tourists come from?" Out of the mouths of babes, her brain still physically developing at age sixteen and without malicious intentional irreverence, Allison said in a very low monotone voice heard only by me, "They certainly did not come up from under the water, awkward, no disrespect."

Seconds later, Allison, with camera in hand, snapped a picture of the United States flag blowing in the wind and in the foreground of just one large cumulus cloud on an otherwise spectacular bright sunny day. As with all digital cameras, you can instantly look at your pictures after shooting them. Upon gazing at this most recent snapshot, to her amazement, the cloud in the background was the eerie likeness of our heavenly father. The cloud seems to resemble the shape of a heavenly father not scolding an irreverent child, but one protecting the souls of the sailors entombed in the *Arizona* beneath the water. Allison captured an image of a magical moment that seemed to stop time and reflect back at another.

During our visit, we met Jerome T. Hagen, retired brigadier general of the United States Marine Corps. Hagen enlisted in the United States Marine Corps in 1952, during the Korean War. He served as a drill sergeant at the San Diego Recruit Depot, completed officer candidate classes, commissioned a second lieutenant, and rose to the grade of brigadier general. He served 483 combat missions in an A4 Skyhawk aircraft during the Vietnam War, earning him the silver-star medal and numerous other decorations.

We bought the book *War in the Pacific*, penned by Brigadier General Hagen, which is about the events of World War II in the Pacific. The book is the best-selling non-fiction book in Hawaii. Brigadier General Hagen signed the book over to my two daughters:

March 15, 2008
Pearl Harbor
To: Amanda and Allison Hubele

This book is in memory of your grandfather, George Hubele, and his service in the U.S. Navy during the Korean War.

Semper Fidelis
Jerome T. Hagen
B. Gen. USMC (retired)

After signing the book, he told us about the two Japanese strikes on Pearl Harbor and that they contemplated a third attack. He told us—information is in the book—of how Combined Fleet Admiral Isoroku Yamamoto of Japan traveled extensively in the United States before World War II. He was the naval attaché in Washington, D.C., and was educated at Harvard, taking language courses. Yamamoto increased his knowledge of American industrial and military capacity while living in the United States.

"Aircraft and midget submarines of the Imperial Japanese Navy began an attack on the United States. Under the command of Admiral Isoroku Yamamoto, the attack was devastating in loss of life and damage to the U. S. fleet. At 6:05 a.m. on December 7, 1941, the six Japanese carriers launched a first wave of 183 planes composed mainly of dive—bombers, horizontal bombers and fighter planes. The Japanese hit American ships and military installations at 7:51 a.m. The first wave attacked military airfields on Ford Island. At 8:30 a.m., a second wave of 170 Japanese planes, mostly torpedo bombers, attacked the fleet anchored in Pearl Harbor. The battleship *Arizona* hit with an armor-piercing bomb, which penetrated the forward ammunition compartment, blowing the ship apart and sinking it within seconds. Overall, nine ships of the U.S. fleet were sunk and twenty-one ships were severely damaged. The overall death toll reached 2,350, including 68 civilians, and 1,178 injured. Of the military personnel lost at Pearl Harbor, 1,177 were from the *Arizona*. The USS *Ward* fired the first shots on a midget submarine that had surfaced outside of Pearl Harbor; the Ward did successfully sink the midget about an hour before the assault on Pearl Harbor." [7]

"Several Japanese junior officers, including Mitsuo Fuchida and Minoru Genda, the chief architect of the attack, urged Japanese leader Nagumo to carry out a third strike in order to destroy much of Pearl Harbor's fuel and torpedo storage, maintenance, and dry dock facilities. Military historians have suggested the destruction of these facilities would have hampered the U.S. Pacific Fleet far more seriously than loss of its battleships." [8]

Nagumo decided against a third strike because of too many risks with returning planes landing at night and running unacceptably low on fuel. He believed the second strike had met the main objective of the mission. Besides, he believed the United States would be ready for another strike, and that would mean many more Japanese losses. The Japanese Navy preferred to practice the conservation of strength instead of the total destruction of the enemy. U.S. Commanders felt that if a third strike had occurred, World War II would have lasted another two years. The lack of any formal declaration of war prior to the attack on Pearl Harbor led President Franklin D. Roosevelt to proclaim "December 7th, 1941—a date which will live in infamy."

While visiting Pearl Harbor, you can also tour the Battleship Missouri Memorial, the home of the most celebrated battleship built by the United States Navy. Walking on the 53,000-square-foot deck, it feels like you are reliving history on the Surrender Deck, where the Japanese commanders surrendered, ending World War II.

When Japan surrendered on September 2, 1945, officially marking the end of World War II with eleven Japanese dignitaries witnessing the event, General MacArthur signed for all the Allies and Admiral Nimitz signed for the United States. Immediately after the signing of the peace agreement, the sky seemed to clear away all the clouds.

After completion of much needed repair work to the USS *Missouri*, it was back into commission during the Korean War. The Missouri fired a salvo of sixteen-inch shells from its turrets while bombarding Chongjin, North Korea in an effort to dismantle enemy communications in October of 1950.

Visiting Pearl Harbor with my daughters is an experience that will forever remain etched in my mind. If Dad had still been alive and able to join us during the visit, his stories of submarine life during the Korean War would have really come to life. His stories about delivering supplies to wartime ships like the USS *Missouri* in the pitch darkness of night and out in the middle of the ocean from an imposing heap of steel submarine mean much more to us now.

During the middle of the week, we visited the Diamond Head Crater, on of Hawaii's most distinctive landmarks. The extinct volcano site is just minutes from Waikiki Beach. Parking at the bottom costs just a few dollars and the long narrow hike is as exhilarating as the breathtaking view at the summit.

In the middle of the Island of Oahu sits the Dole Plantation. The plantation is a tribute to the role that the pineapple business played in the development of the island. The pineapple garden maze is two miles of manicured paths, recognized as the world's largest maze, according to the *1998 Guinness Book of Records*.

On the second to last day of our trip to Oahu, we drove a rental car to the spectacular views of the North Shore, a five-mile stretch of beaches where surfing became legendary. Sunset Beach, Waimea Bay Beach, and Ehukai Beach make up the collection of beaches known as the "Banzai Pipeline." Waves can reach as high as twenty-five feet, attracting wave-riders and spectators from around the world in hopes of catching that perfect wave. The beautiful North Shore is truly an unspoiled section of Oahu.

On the last day of our trip, before we had to board the airplane to return home, we drove our rental car from our hotel on Waikiki Beach to the north-central part of the island in search of the Polynesian Cultural Center. Upon arriving at the center, Hawaiian dancers place leis over the heads of visitors and lead them down walkways past towering waterfalls, grass huts, coconut trees, and native fern plants for dinner and a luau. Being presented with a flower lei is probably one of the most enjoyable and unforgettable Hawaiian customs. It is considered rude to remove a lei once it is accepted in view of everyone, especially in view of the person who gave it to you.

We encountered many foods with names that seemed foreign to us. Bread made with mashed ripe bananas was a favorite at our table, as the servers refilled our basket several times. Mahimahi, a white, sweet moderately dense fish tasted great and baked to perfection. We ate taro leaves as a vegetable in our salad, and the leaves wrapped around the fish and meats that cooked on a fire. We ate *lomi* salmon, which is a cold dish made with diced salmon, tomatoes, and onion. Guava cakes made from bananas and coconuts serve many at most luaus on the island. *Kulolo* is another pudding desert made with taro, brown sugar, and coconut milk.

By far one of the highlights of our trip, the Polynesian Cultural Center, is a gorgeous authentic luau setting where native Hawaiians tell a real story. The young men perform a fire-and-dance routine and the young women dance the night away as they perform a Tahitian dance competition. The "Ha Breath of Life" is a spectacular story about a saga of passion ignited by fire, song, dance, and a family washed ashore by volcanic destruction.

The Hawaiian culture is fascinating, lively, colorful, and unique. During our weeklong stay, we enjoyed the fabulous one-of-a-kind sunsets, the surf, and the clean sandy beaches, but the culture is what truly makes the Hawaiian Islands a special, unforgettable place.

The memories of this spectacle will last longer than any suntan you could get on the beach.

The memories remain.

"EDUCATION"

Four years before getting married, Mom graduated from Laboure High School in 1948, ranked third in a class of eighty-five students, which carried as its reward an offer of a scholarship to St. Louis University, an offer she never accepted, opting to take care of her father who had cancer.

After two years of high school, Dad joined the navy. Though he received his GED in the navy, he often proclaimed that he had a degree from the University of Hard Knocks. Though maybe Mom and Dad did not reach for their full potential for themselves, they each knew of the importance of an education that they wanted for their children. This chapter evolved from lessons learned from my parents as a child about the importance of an education, from thoughts written down during several years as a teacher, and to the curiosity of how to try to make things better at school.

Nothing is more important than the education of our children. A large part of our attitude toward things, conditioned by opinions and emotions, we unconsciously absorb as children from our environment. We rarely reflect on this powerful influence that tradition has on our conscious thought, convictions, and ways we choose to live our lives. Albert Einstein wrote, "Words are and remain an empty sound, and the road to perdition (loss of your soul) has ever been accompanied by lip service to an ideal. Personalities are not formed by what is heard and said, but by labor and activity, by doing." Students learn more by doing and being active participants rather than passive listeners.

The most important method of education always has consisted of that in which the student desires to participate. This applies to the first attempts at writing, solving mathematical problems, learning lines for a play, practicing new techniques for a sport, or writing a doctor's thesis for graduation from an accredited university.

Motivation, the foundation of every effort, exists behind every achievement. Educational methods are best when teacher and student have a heightened interest and a desire for truth and understanding of the subject matter.

The worst type of educational approach works with methods of fear, force, and authority. Such methods destroy the self-confidence, creativity, and self-expression of the student. The development of general ability for independent thinking and judgment is foremost, not the acquisition of specialized knowledge. If a person masters the fundamentals of his subject and learns to think and work independently, he will surely find his way and will be able to better adapt himself to progress to changes than the person whose training principally consists in the acquiring of detailed knowledge.

What skills do we teach our children? Are we preparing and educating our children for the future? Should we at least teach students to achieve excellent standards in core academic subjects? How do we answer these aforementioned questions and still address all aspects of the costs to operate a school?

Little improvement takes place in schools unless leaders attend to the problems of the community. Before schools can make significant change, communities need jobs and training programs, so all workers earn a living wage and are able to get or afford health insurance for their families. If we are to take a serious effort to improve our public schools in major cities, safe affordable housing must be available to families. We must repair or tear down all abandoned houses in the city and replace them with new homes.

In most schools, curriculum is determined by textbooks and by vague guidelines established by state and local authorities. The mere act of revising a curriculum each year, and then combining it with expectations, is bound to bring some improvement. The mere fact of paying close attention to curriculum makes a mediocre school better. Physical education, art, music, creativity, and imagination are essential parts of the curriculum. The stimulation of the artistic part of the brain complements quite nicely the steady focus needed in math, science, and analytical thinking. Physical education became the norm in schools after the First World War raised concerns about the fitness of our soldiers. With so many overweight children today, physical education is just as important today.

Developing a curriculum means doing research on it, then evaluating it, then implementing it and revising it every year. Is it more important to know about the French Revolution or to prepare students to get through the sociological problems of childhood in the United States of America? The numbers of hours of each school day are set. If you add something new to the curriculum, then something else has to be shorter or deleted.

In order for quality teacher instruction to occur, schools must have a strong professional development program to train teachers in methodologies proven to work. School facilities must be adequately equipped for technology and modern methods of teaching. With technology, so much more material is available at students' immediate disposal.

It is much easier to make one great school than to make one great school system. However, inspired people can achieve great things where others have given up. A gifted principal hires talented teachers.

The teachers involve the parents to keep a close eye on their children's education. Setting up a Web site to monitor grades and homework in all classes on a daily basis facilitates parents' involvement and open communications with teachers via e-mail. Some high schools are beginning to see the importance of linking some advanced computer technology programs to nearby junior colleges, as partners to ready students for more advanced studies. High expectations and a professional spirit among the teachers ensure successful practices at school, a rich sense of community, and uncompromising ambition. An effective model, with highly qualified administrators and teachers in place, creates a link with parents and a more effective way to reach the students.

In order to rally a school around a set of objectives, it is necessary for teachers, parents, and students to feel a sense of community, taking stock of its current situation—the good things and the obstacles. If parents and students are required to work eight hours of school community service per month per individual, turning any school into a successful community is a reachable goal. Parent committees focusing on safety, lunch programs, cleanup, recycling, maintenance help, painting, data entry, organizing book orders, hall monitoring, field trips, fundraising, concessions at sporting events, commencement, and many other activities help raise the standards to empower schools with a sense of community. Beautifying the school simply by filling walls with photographs and students' works greatly adds to the learning environment.

It is my contention that we need to be less concerned with teaching "content" and more concerned with teaching "development." With computer technology today, students sometimes feel bombarded with knowledge and content. However, students are able to print or save relevant information and go back for repeated review. Laptop computers, mainstream in many school classrooms, are emerging in many public schools. Across the country, school districts in all states are seeing a boom in one-to-one laptop programs. Schools in today's day and age are doing their students an injustice without considering a one-to-one laptop program. Computers loaded with textbook and Internet software allow teachers to give lessons with interactive worksheets, and allow students to access to the Internet for real-world research to illustrate their lessons and heighten their learning curve. Tests taken online and calculated by the computer show the results, which are available immediately.

Schools by their very nature are expressions of opinion—which certain things to teach our children—and philosophers have been debating these issues since the time of Plato. The Quakers of England discussed ways to improve their schools in the seventeenth century and, at the same time, tried to keep individual religious beliefs separate and personal. John Dewey created not only a school but also an entire movement based on his vision of child development. When George W. Bush became president, he started the program "No Child Left Behind." Some people feel that President Bush created another level of unproductive wasteful spending, with too much money spent on bureaucracy and not enough spent on instruction in the classroom. President Bush has received much criticism for spending so much money on the war and not enough on educational instruction, but without the protection of our democracy, our schools would not enjoy the freedoms of choice we have today.

Many of the same issues of yesteryear are issues argued today, such as money, taxes, class size, budget, curriculum, safety, teacher-student ratio, extra-curricular activities, religion, dress code, lunch program, and many other important issues.

Any effort to improve academic achievement starts at home. It is wrong information to hear that the government, the media, and the nation's teachers—with no mention of the role of parents—cause the plight of our children. Parents are the major fabric of the school; they influence students more than the administrators or the teachers. Parents can help raise the academic standards of their children by supporting teachers, expanding the use of computers and technology at home, staying involved with homework, and monitoring the progress of their children. Parents help by encouraging their children to find something that they excel in, whether it is a sport, art, music, writing, or some other activity; they learn and have fun at the same time. Hands-on activities help increase self-esteem in other aspects of the students' lives.

If parents need literacy assistance, then parenting assistance needs to be the issue addressed first. The Missouri Partnership for Parenting Assistance and Literacy Investment for Tomorrow is a broad-based statewide parent education and literacy assistance program. Most states have adopted a similar program. It is very important that we make sure that our parents are educated so that they can help with the education of their children.

Parents must help children deal more effectively with peer pressure. Parents, who build a strong relationship with their children, so they have a solid foundation, make sure their children are productive members of the family. Sometimes it is better to listen to our children, instead of trying to solve all their problems for them. By encouraging children to make good decisions and acknowledging successes, parents set healthy boundaries and help prepare them for challenging situations.

Administrators must eliminate the know-it-all and bury-our-heads-in-the-sand attitudes and remember that taxpaying parents pay their salaries. Administrators and teachers need to reach out and wrap their arms around problems in order to create the kind of change schools need. They need to not only make parents and students aware of grades and policies, but also show the student what he or she can do to improve. In turn, if administrators stop listening to the opinions of out-of-state consulting firms and paying for money-influenced studies, they will have more time to give the same amount of credence to those who know the students best: the parents.

Because approximately 85 percent of a public school's budget is mandated by either the state or federal government, in order to meet the criteria to maintain accreditation, school administrators need to devote sufficient amounts of time and effort researching federal and state funding, incentive grants, and community support programs. Wise school administrators appoint and hire a teacher to the special position of chief academic officer as a curriculum monitor to help keep students and teachers focused on staying on task, improving grades and test scores. Some school districts hire additional instructors from Teach for America, a program that recruits recent college graduates to teach in deprived communities. Many times, young teachers bring an energy level and enthusiasm that is contagious to more tenured older teachers.

Major projects such as building a skyscraper or a school usually start out simply by creating a plan. When setting policy for our schools, we must clarify where problems exist and what issues are the most pressing. This should be one of our government's biggest roles. If our government can set the policy standard, then our administrators at the state and local school district levels, can take the next step in improving schools and raising expectations of our students. One school district's reporting of expenditures per student may only include instructional money spent, while another district's may also include administrative costs and prorated monies spent on building improvements. When reporting financial statements to federal and state governments, schools need to report information in a uniform manner, according to statutes, rules, and regulations. Obviously, other information is necessary to paint an accurate picture of a school, but comparable and reliable data is necessary to make informed decisions about which schools to entrust with our children's education.

School boards of education are accountable for a budget that is honest and fair, showing how much money they need and how they want to spend the money. Any board of education's responsibility is to focus on increasing performance, increasing quality faculty retention, growing the use of valuable computer technology, improving building facilities, getting value for school district expenditures, developing advanced and special needs programs, funding extracurricular activities, and increasing discipline of students (meaning better-prepared students, not punishing them). Their focus is to rid schools of drugs and violence, increase graduation rate, eliminate illiteracy, restore our world ranking in science and math, and promoting the significance of college-level classes completed during high school years for college credit. School boards that are aggressive in marketing their district's visibility and name brand, stand a great chance of increasing community involvement and interaction that brings needed new energy and bright new creative ideas. By addressing these issues, standardized test scores will increase.

Corporations in every community must pay their fair share to the tax base. Big corporations that finance their operations through tax-increment financing (TIF) and funny money programs, making record profits year after year, deny tax proceeds to public schools in the neighborhoods that they do business. Missouri law requires that 25 percent of state tax revenue go to public schools. Citizens need to demand that these big corporations not use unfair loopholes to the tax system that shortchanges our public school systems. Without these tax proceeds, schools cannot renovate old school buildings and build new ones. With more help from small businesses and large corporations, employers recoup benefits later, because they can hire students trained to reason, communicate, analyze, and solve problems.

If taxpayers are serious about improving our communities and helping our educators provides a good education for our children, then taxpayers must provide the hands-on community service, fiscal support, and stability required to bring about the improvements proposed. Every school must promote partnerships that increase parental involvement and participation in promoting the social, emotional, and academic growth of children.

At an early age, students need to learn the value of money. They need to be taught a class about balancing a checkbook, saving money, and investing for the future. Warren Buffet's book *Snowball* is about learning a business sense at an early age, building networking relationships, saving money, and investing. The financial crisis of 2009 and President Obama's healthcare reform issues have provided unique teaching opportunities to talk about finding answers at the individual level.

Receiving an allowance for chores around the house remains a valid approach to earning and saving money. The next step is planning what to do with the money. The importance of learning to invest in stocks and bonds can become a lifelong habit. Children can learn about some of their favorite companies and that it is possible to buy shares in those companies when they are older. With the plethora of stock-trading Web sites, students have many opportunities to learn; besides, they love to navigate on the computer. Learning about children's favorite companies, such as Nike, J. C. Penney's, McDonald's, GameStop, Best Buy, Kellogg's, AT&T, and Twitter, help to develop a mind with a business sense. (Jack Dorsey, cofounder of Twitter, is a native of St. Louis and attended the University of Missouri at Rolla for three years.)

Students need to realize that they forfeit their chance for life at its fullest when they do not give their best effort at school. When students give a minimum effort to learning, they get a minimum of opportunities in return. Even with parents' help and teachers' best efforts, in the end, the students' effort determine how much and how well they learn. With a determined effort, students attain the knowledge and skills to control their own destiny. By learning to study with self-discipline, students become lifelong learners able to apply their talents with high expectations and able to turn challenges into opportunities.

Many school systems have attempted sweeping reforms over past decades, but may not be adequately addressing our quickly changing computerized society. Because the MySpace and Facebook Web sites are fearful to many adults due to some of the improprieties taken by some Web users, the younger generation uses these sites in their daily lives, communicating with friends, connecting about homework, organizing study groups, doing business, and finding out about social events. Students who use these sites wisely and learn time management improve their study habits and do a better job with homework. When studying, it is best to establish a routine for homework time and limiting distractions by finding a quiet location away from the phone, television, MP3 players and iPods. It helps to divide assignments into smaller, more manageable parts. By keeping an assignment calendar, including all work due dates and test dates, students stay organized day to day.

Though good grades are important, it is not recommended that high school students give up all extracurricular activities in order to concentrate on getting all As. When students pass up opportunities to try healthy new experiences, they shortchange their personalities as well as their life experiences. It is important to do well academically, but at the same time, enjoy a well-rounded life. Colleges value applicants that demonstrate an active role in extracurricular activities because well-rounded young adults are more likely to succeed in college and in life.

More must be done to ensure every school in the United States be free of drugs, violence, and the presence of firearms and alcohol in the hands of children. A safe environment allows teachers to work in a disciplined environment conducive to learning. Safety is the number one priority at every school. We must fight to bring organization, academic excellence, and clean bathrooms to all schools. Schools are about teaching our children in a safe and clean environment with the best possible teachers. Certainly, safety rules and procedures, at all schools, are important in today's environment. Good relationships, with mutual respect between teachers and students have a greater impact on safety than any other factors. Programs that stress zero tolerance for fighting are important and there must be assurance that, during troubling situations, authorities will follow through in a proper manner.

Today, every school safety program must address Internet safety to include filtering Internet content, monitoring secure files, blocking inappropriate Web sites, prohibiting misuse of e-mails, restricting instant messaging, following cyberspace etiquette, and securing student online protection. When it comes to computer security, schools have the same needs as any large business corporation. To help in this security area, when schools collaborate with CDW-G Corporation, they get one of the best values for their technology dollars, including an extensive range of services from assessment, design, implementation, and computer support services for K-12 schools. After comparing the norms established at hundreds of other schools, CDW-G can customize a security program for any school.

School lunch programs are important because our children's health is important. Nearly one in five children is obese, a figure that has tripled since 1985. Successful school lunch programs must strip some of the fat, high-fructose corn syrup, preservatives, hydrogenated oils and sugars from the menu; ban unhealthy vending machines; and introduce more healthy portions of fresh fruits and vegetables. The Center of Disease Control and Prevention predicts 30 percent of our elementary grade school children will develop diabetes unless we change trends in school lunch programs. Government lunch guidelines and food corporations only interested in profits do not change eating behaviors of students. Health teachers, nutritionists, dieticians, and parents must give children the tools, knowledge, and food vocabulary, so they make the right choices themselves.

There is more to nutrition than just healthy bones and strong muscles; there is food for the brain, too. Some successful school districts get local chefs from four—or five-star restaurants to volunteer a few hours each month to help with the menu and prepare healthy lunches. Good food, with the right combination of protein, dietary vitamin values, grains, fresh fruits, and vegetables give students more energy. Feed our children great lunches and they will learn more and be smarter.

Shortly after moving into the White House, Michelle Obama started growing a vegetable garden instead of a rose garden. She started this program in hopes of having a vegetable garden at every school in hopes of showing children how to eat healthy foods.

Most states require all students to take and pass three years of English, mathematics, science, and social studies. It is now a standard policy to recommend that students take two years of computer technology and at least two years of foreign language classes in high school. Everyone needs to know how to articulate, write, count, get around, and have a general idea how most things work. For these reasons, the teaching of general core subjects remains part of American culture, in addition to test scores showing much room for nationwide improvement.

Improving test scores does not necessarily mean that children learn more; it just means they are better prepared for a standardized way of measurement. Teachers can fall into a trap by not teaching what they know works, afraid they will not be politically correct or in vogue with the current hot teaching style. If teachers substantially boost the overall classroom performance and develop an appreciation for learning of all students, then they have succeeded at educational reform.

In the old days, discipline problems meant speaking out of turn or getting caught chewing bubble gum. Schools have much more serious issues today. There is a lot wrong with our schools, but most of the problems come from external influences. It is no wonder that many schools cannot solve their problems; we are doing things backward. We must first solve the external problems schools face. The schools have not failed; we have failed the schools. There are many ways to save them.

In 1964, undergraduate women at Harvard University could not use the main library until their junior year of studies. Today, the campus has seventy-two libraries that are available to all Harvard students of many diverse cultures from around the world and even their first female president took office on July 1, 2007. Her name is Drew Gilpin Faust, a history scholar and talented administrator, who has strong restructuring, finance, and fundraising skills. By studying the models of some of the most successful institutions of higher learning, though we cannot duplicate all their strategies, we can learn from them.

The most common problems faced by teachers from 1940 through 1970 included talking out of turn, chewing gum, note-passing, making noise, reading comic books, running in the halls, breaking dress code, not turning in homework, and damaging school materials. Today, teachers encounter problems such as absenteeism, drug abuse, alcohol abuse, pregnancy, vandalism, guns, violence, robbery, gangs, sexual diseases, AIDS, abortion, suicide, and murder. Society's problems not only affect but also infect our schools. Our classrooms are overwhelmed with sociological problems and a growing burden on our teachers to get everything right. We expect our teachers to be doctors, social workers, psychologists, and family counselors, a reality in our school systems today. Ridding our schools of drugs, alcohol, and violence is a good start to saving our schools.

"If an unfriendly power had attempted to impose on America the mediocre educational performance that exists today, we might well have viewed it as an act of war. As it stands, we have allowed this to happen to ourselves. We have dismantled essential support systems, which helped make gains possible. We have in effect, been committing an act of unthinking unilateral educational disarmament." These statements, published by the United States Department of Education's National Commission appeared in a report called "Excellence in Education, a Nation at Risk: The Imperative For Educational Reform," as far back as 1983. [9]

Making significant changes that make a school better, life better, the world a better place to live, is more important than just being successful. Working together, the connection between businesses, administrators, educators, parents, and children must continue as a strong foundation in our communities. Quality schools help to maintain the value of our community, maintain the values of homes, and provide a safe environment in which to raise our families and help our businesses prosper.

Most people understand the relevance of education. To act intelligently in the human affairs of the school district is only possible if an attempt is made to understand the thoughts, motives, and apprehensions of all people involved so fully that one can see the world through their eyes. All well-meaning people should try to contribute as much as possible to improve such mutual understanding. For the system of education and free enterprise to work, a healthy balance between educating students to be productive and the purchasing power they attain later by working must be achieved. Somewhere between the light of this truth and the darkness of deceit is the place all of us choose to live our lives. It is time we recognize all the burdens for what they are and how they contribute to all the problems in our schools and how outside influences affect our schools. We reach the goal of being happy when each person makes an intellectual effort together with a striving self, and with creative activities or hobbies and work that adds meaning to life. A good education gives people the tools to solve problems. Working together, the people living in the community can fix problems in the local school district, overcoming the burdens holding back education.

Parents and teachers are responsible for instilling in students with knowing the importance of applying themselves and obtaining a good education. The only people who knock a good education are people who do not have one.

The memories of my school days remain.

"DANGEROUS WATERS"

A man brings his beautiful wife a full glass of water and two aspirins. She looks surprised and says, "I do not have a headache." The husband says, "Aha!" Maybe the wife just did not want to drink the water.

The Great Flood of 1993 constituted the most costly and devastating flood to do damage in the United States in modern history. Unlike spring snowmelt flooding, which allows time for flood forecasting, the unusual and extreme amounts of rain during the summer of 1993 allowed very little time for advance flood warnings. Levees gave way, farmlands washed out, thousands of homes and businesses were ruined, roads were destroyed, water was contaminated, and people died. Losses estimated at over twenty billion dollars changed the landscape of millions of acres in Middle America.

An image of a large white two-story farmhouse floating down the Mississippi River made national news. Sunset Lakes Golf Course was completely submerged underwater except for the greens that looked like giant water lily pads floating in the Meramec River. Much of the Chesterfield Valley Business District was completely underwater, shutting off access to the bridge crossing over the Missouri River.

In July of 1993, my daughter Amanda, nine years old at the time, joined me as we decided to spend a weekend sandbagging on the banks of the River des Peres, near Gravois Road and only four miles from our home, where it flowed through the southern edge of the city of St. Louis near the municipality of Lemay. The River des Peres is a river basin runoff that flows away from the Mississippi River, one of the largest water drainage watersheds in the region. We drove to this location and joined hundreds of other volunteers working around the clock to reinforce two miles of non-federal levee along the River des Peres waterway.

On the previous weekend, emergency management officials and police evacuated two hundred families from the areas we were working, in fear that the rising waters would isolate them. The Army Corp of Engineers supplied volunteers with mounds of sand, shovels, work gloves, bags, and rolls of plastic.

Operation Clean Stream of St. Louis is one of the longest and largest ongoing river restoration projects in the country. The annual August event attracts nearly two thousand volunteers each year to the Meramec River and its tributaries to help clean up the river.

Floodwaters give the false impression that there is an abundance of clean water when actually just the opposite is true. Floods contaminate much of the water.

After the flood of 1993, drastic amounts of water dumped mega-tons more trash and debris than any previous years. Thousands more volunteers were needed for cleanup that year, because the Mississippi and Meramec Rivers flooded several miles past their banks for long stretches throughout several states in the middle of America. Rebuilding of levees and relocation efforts went on for several years after the flood of 1993, but efforts must continue to ensure cleaner rivers and safe drinking water for everyone. No living things can survive without safe water.

Everyone remembers the television coverage of the man holding up the voting ballot with the dangling chads under the light during the presidential election between George W. Bush and Al Gore. The notion of this man hired to count votes for such an important event of this magnitude seemed wrong, since he had bad eyesight, wore very thick glasses, and seemed cross-eyed. Though Bush won and did some good things as our president, he was not a good environmentalist president. Big oil spills were too frequent, pollution laws were too lax, and not enough was done to help flood recovery efforts such as Katrina during his administration. Al Gore went on to win a Pulitzer prize for his work on the human causes of global warming and pollution that are disrupting the environment.

St. Louis, Missouri, residents pay about a nickel for the use of one hundred cubic feet of water. The Missouri American Water Company maintains about 4,200 miles of water mains and 31,000 fire hydrants in St. Louis County. Since 2007, the water company has been toting infrastructure improvements, improved service reliability, enhanced fire protection, and a heightened integrity of our water systems. Cleaning up our oceans, lakes, rivers, and streams should be at the top of the agenda at all local, state, and federal levels. Stiff fines accessed to those companies or individuals that pollute our waters and necessary changes to fix those problems must be in place and monitored thereafter to keep our waters safe.

In recent decades, there has been a decrease in the percentage of rivers having top quality water. There are several sources of water pollution that reduce the overall quality of water in the rivers across America. Industry discharges liquid waste products, and insecticides and pesticides drain from soil on farmlands into our rivers. Serious oil spills or toxic chemical accidents are events that make the national news, but just one gallon of insecticide can kill as many as a thousand fish in a river. Rain falling through polluted air absorbs air pollutants as it falls to the ground. Car engines burning gasoline results in pollutants such as sulphur dioxide and nitrogen oxide spewing into the air. Much industrial waste discharged into water are mixtures of chemicals. Some of these problematic chemical waste is so toxic, making them difficult to handle and expensive to find solutions. Some companies try to cut costs of safely disposing of waste by illegally dumping chemicals at times and in places where authorities will not catch them. Many companies do not have their parking lots cleaned, allowing trash and debris to wash down sewer drains.

England's first water pollution act of 1388 made it illegal to dump garbage into rivers. Anyone breaking that law in those days faced hanging. Today in the United States, the Environmental Protection Agency is supposed to protect our water resources, but they are not doing enough to ensure that everyone respects the water environment.

Thousands of pollution incidents are going undetected and unreported every month in America, causing problems for plants, wildlife, and humans.

During a flood, all the chemicals used in a household end up washed into our rivers and streams. Petrol, diesel fuel, antifreeze, bleach, medical waste, human waste, acids, alcohols, and a host of other chemicals wash out of homes, businesses, factories, refineries, hospitals, and other buildings.

After the barbarians destroyed Europe's ancient culture, a better cultural life slowly began to form from two sources: the bible and a water system.

In many parts of Africa and India, getting clean water is still a crisis and a central preoccupation of daily lives of people. In poor rural areas of these two countries, people can spend five hours per day walking back and forth just to get water. Time looking for water leads to lack of time working, which leads to poverty, which leads to hunger. "Over a billion people on our planet will never have a clean drink of water. There are 2.5 billion people in the world without toilet facilities." [10]

Remembering a quote from Dad in 2003: "Never thought the day would come where people pay two dollars for a bottle of water, but it is understandable in today's world."

"CARDINALS BASEBALL"

For decades, St. Louis residents have shared a year-round hobby of talking baseball, specifically talking about the St. Louis Cardinals baseball team. Professional baseball is a results-oriented and perception-based game. America's favorite pastime is the same great game that it has always been in ballparks across the country.

The St. Louis Cardinals "birds on the bat" trademark is arguably the best logo in Major League Baseball. It has been a mainstay on Cardinals' jerseys since 1922, except for a one-year hiatus in 1956 when the team went with "Cardinals" in plain script lettering across the front of the jerseys. Maybe the reason for the change was to save money, but it was a dumb decision, because a large majority of fans protested and the following year the team went back to the logo.

Jesse Burkett is probably the least-known great hitter in baseball history. He grew up in the same town Stan Musial would later be born, Scranton, Pennsylvania. In 1901, playing for the St. Louis Cardinals, Burkett led the National League in batting average (.376), runs scored (142), and hits (226). He batted over .400 two times in his career. Major League Baseball inducted Burkett into the Hall of Fame in 1946.

After limited playing time in his first year of professional baseball, Rogers Hornsby decided he needed to get stronger if he was going to have any hope of a long career. He spent the entire winter enduring extremely difficult labor on his uncle's farm. The hard work on the farm paid huge dividends. When asked, "What do you do in the winter when there is no baseball?" Hornsby replied, "I stare out the window and wait for spring." We know that statement is not true, but that is how much he loved the game of baseball.

Hornsby's career batting average of .358 is the highest by a right-handed hitter in the history of Major League Baseball. He is the only right-handed hitter in the twentieth century to hit .400 in three seasons. He is the only player ever to win the National League Triple Crown two times. The Associated Press voted him onto the Major League Baseball All-Century Team as a second baseman.

"I do not want to play golf. When I hit a ball, I want someone else to go chase it," says Hornsby. [11] This statement is tame and much less mean-spirited compared to some other written accusations of the man. "By some historical accounts of the time, Rogers Hornsby was meaner than Ty Cobb and suspicions surfaced that Hornsby was a member of the Klu Klux Klan, according to baseball writer Fred Lieb." [12] Though the Cardinals' organization retired his number, character issues have seemed to squash mentions of his playing days by the media. However, sportswriters elected Rogers Hornsby as a first ballot Hall of Fame inductee in 1942.

"The doctors x-rayed my head and found nothing."

Quote by Dizzy Dean

"You were attracted by the graceful rhythm of his pitching motion; the long majestic sweep of his arm as he let the baseball fly; the poised alertness after the pitch. That was what counted and you knew it when batter after batter swung ineptly at pitches they couldn't even see."

Quote by Editor of New York Times, about Dizzy Dean

"As a ballplayer, Dizzy Dean was a natural phenomenon, like the Grand Canyon or the Great Barrier Reef. Nobody ever taught him baseball and he never had to learn. He was just doing what came naturally when a scout named Dan Curtis discovered him on a Texas sandlot and gave him his first contract."

Quote by Red Smith

The Chicago Cubs and St. Louis Cardinals are arguably the best rivals in Major League Baseball. Jay Hanna, "Dizzy Dean," is one of the few players that experienced both sides of that rivalry. In the 1934 World Series, pitcher Dizzy won two games and his brother, pitcher Paul "Daffy" Dean won the two other games to bring the championship home to St. Louis. Dizzy's career in Chicago lacked the flare he showed in St. Louis due to an injury he suffered in the all-star game of 1934. A line drive hit off the bat of Earl Averill broke his toe. Dean altered his pitching motion to compensate for the broken toe, injuring his throwing arm in the process. Soon after that, he retired from playing baseball.

Dizzy Dean, great Cardinals pitcher who once won thirty games in one season, after retiring became an announcer for the American League St. Louis Browns. During a dismal season for the Browns, Dean proclaimed that he could still pitch better than the Browns' pitchers. The Browns organization gave him an opportunity in the last game of the season. Dean pitched four scoreless innings and hit a single in his only plate appearance.

Sportswriters elected Dizzy Dean into the Hall of Fame in 1953.

You cannot write a digest about the history of the St. Louis Cardinals baseball team without mentioning Stan "The Man" Musial. Stan, the greatest Cardinals player of all time, was honored with a dedication of a bigger-than-life statue in regard for his great play and determination standing outside the new Busch Stadium in St. Louis, just as it stood outside old Busch Stadium.

It was not an easy start for Stan. Stan, at age seventeen (1938), began his career as a pitcher for a Cardinal farm team called the Daytona Beach Islanders. When he was not pitching, he sometimes played outfield. During a game in 1940, playing centerfield for the Islanders, he dove for a sinking line drive injuring his pitching shoulder and ending his pitching career. Here he was, a devastated young man from a steel-mill town in Pennsylvania, thinking about returning home to get a job in the mills.

Manager of the Islanders, Dickie Kerr, saw enough in Stan's hitting ability to urge him to continue playing baseball as an outfielder. One day, Branch Richey, the head of the St. Louis Cardinals organization, came out to watch Stan play centerfield. Legend has it that he only needed to watch Stan bat once. Richey was so impressed with his left-handed style that before the season ended, Musial was playing for the major league team. He moved quickly through the minors, Daytona to Springfield, to Rochester, and finally to the big show in St. Louis. During those weeks of his first year as a major leaguer, he batted an amazing .426 for the Cardinals.

During World War II, since most of the major leaguers went off to war, many younger players took their place until they came back. Fifteen-year-old Joe Nuxhall, the youngest player to pitch in the major leagues, pitched for the Cincinatti Reds. If not for the summer seasons they did not play while serving their country, what kind of stats would Stan Musial and Ted Williams have accumulated playing baseball?

Over several years after returning from the war, Stan did so well when playing against the Brooklyn Dodgers and New York Giants that the east coast fans gave him the nickname Stan "The Man" Musial. "The best way to pitch to Stan Musial is to walk him and try to pick him off first base."—Joe Garagiola

Musial, with a 175-pound frame, stayed quiet in his stance, but like a corkscrew and with perfect timing, he turned his hips and shoulders to generate power and unleash a fury of hits against National League pitchers. During his career, Stan led the National League in batting seven times, won three most valuable player awards, had 3,630 hits and 475 homers, and averaged .331 during a twenty-two season career.

At the time of his retirement from baseball, Musial's total of 3,630 hits and 1,949 runs scored were second only to those of Ty Cobb. He set a major league record with 1,377 extra-base hits. His baseball statistics, likeable style, and class as a human being made him a first-ballot Hall of Famer. Following his playing career—all twenty-two years spent with the St. Louis Cardinals—Stan directed the president's physical fitness program from 1964 through 1967.

Kids who batted right-handed tried to turn around and bat left-handed just to be like Stan. Fathers told stories about Stan and used him as a role model. Coaches taught their players about playing as a team, often citing examples of Stan's character in a recent game.

Some of life's most exciting findings happen by accident or just by overcoming hurdles to get there. One of baseball's all-time greatest hitters would have never realized his talents had it not been for the turning point injury following the diving catch on that fateful night in 1940.

The stories and memories with my dad of watching Stan play and hit home runs over the thirty-three-foot-high right field screen at Sportsman's Park during the late fifties and early sixties will forever remain etched in my brain.

Stan Musial played in many all-star games, but the most renowned all-star game ever played in St. Louis was held at the new Busch Memorial Stadium on July 12, 1966. Cardinals' catcher Tim McCarver scored the winning run on a hit by Maury Wills of the Dodgers in the bottom of the tenth inning to give the National League team a 2 to 1 victory in front of nearly fifty thousand baseball fans. However, it was the sizzling heat (115 degree temperatures on the field) that made this particular game such a memorable event. Asked about the new Busch Memorial Stadium after the game, the legendary Casey Stengel said, "It certainly does hold the heat well." [13]

Not many people know that the famous St. Louis Cardinals' pitcher was born with the name Pack Gibson, after his father who died three months before his birth. Gibson changed his name to Robert when he was eighteen years old. Despite a childhood full of health problems, including asthma, a heart murmur, pneumonia, and rickets, he excelled in sports, especially basketball and baseball. An outstanding high school athlete, Gibson earned a basketball scholarship to Creighton University. In 1957, he signed a contract to play baseball with the St. Louis Cardinals, but delayed his start with the organization for a year, playing professional basketball with the Harlem Globetrotters.

On July 15, 1967, a line drive off the bat of perennial all-star Roberto Clemente of the Pittsburgh Pirates hit Bob Gibson and broke his leg. It is ironic how one of the best free-swinging power hitters of all time broke the leg of one of the best hard-throwing power pitchers of all time. The broken leg put Gibson on the disabled list, but he made a remarkable recovery and, just two months later, returned to finishing the season as the premiere pitcher for the Cardinals and winning the 1967 World Series.

Ernie Banks of the Chicago Cubs coined the phrase "Let's play two," because he loved playing baseball so much. Dad and I loved going to Busch Stadium to watch a doubleheader, especially when the Los Angeles Dodgers came to town. We enjoyed watching great pitching duels between Bob Gibson and Ray Washburn versus Sandy Koufax and Don Drysdale, always low-run scoring affairs. Even watching a double-header still did not seem to be enough baseball; we hated to leave the ballpark.

Thousands of Major League Baseball games are played each year, but something always happens that makes each game unique from the next game. One vivid account of Jack Buck and Mike Shannon calling the game stands out in my memory. Though at the time they were announcing the Cardinals' game, they both started recalling what happened earlier in the evening at a minor league game. A minor league umpire kicked out the organist at the ballpark for playing "Three Blind Mice" at the start of the game, as the umpires came walking on to the field. The telling of this event supplied laughter to baseball fans everywhere as the story was repeated many times at office watercoolers. Buck's class and dry sense of humor along with Shannon's gruff laughter and country-boy style always added flair to their storytelling between innings or before and after the game.

In a movie called *Summer Under the Stars*, Gene Hackman and William DeFoe play FBI agents investigating crimes by the Ku Klux Klan against blacks in Southern Mississippi in the 1960s. In a scene depicting Gene Hackman watching baseball on television, Bob Gibson was pitching against Ron Hunt of the New York Mets in a close 2 to 1 game. Even in this short cameo appearance, with his powerful long strides and determined follow-through, it is evident that Gibson is one of the best at his trade. Ron Hunt was notorious for leaning out over the plate and letting the ball hit him, so he could advance to first base. Year after year, Hunt led the league in being hit by errant balls thrown by pitchers, except balls thrown by Gibson. If Gibson's veracious fastball was a little inside, all batters, including Ron Hunt, tried to get out of the way.

Gibson's 1968 season was so successful that his dominant pitching performances are widely cited in Major League Baseball's decision to lower the pitcher's mound by five inches to make things easier for the hitters. His 1968 season included fifteen wins in a row and a 1.12 earned run average per game. Not afraid to throw inside, his pinpoint control allowed him to throw an overpowering brushback pitch that intimidated the hitters. He was the dominant National League pitcher of the 1960s. Bob Gibson said in a newspaper interview, "His three middle fingers on his hands, oddly, are the same length and that may affect the movement of the ball and the ability to generate so much velocity."

Over his entire career, he collected 251 wins and posted a 2.91 earned run average over seventeen seasons. He won two Cy Young Awards (1968 and 1970), the award given to the league's best pitcher each year. He also won the Most Valuable Player Award in 1968, the award given to the league's best player each year. For nine consecutive years, he won a Gold Glove Award, the award given to the best in fielding excellence at each position on the baseball diamond.

Though most pitchers are weak hitters, Gibson batted .303 one year and was used extensively as a pinch hitter on days he did not pitch. He even hit two home runs in World Series play.

Also, because many younger ballplayers and younger people in general have a sense of entitlement, Gibson has teamed with Reggie Jackson to write a baseball book called *Sixty Feet, Six Inches* for those interested in what happened and what came before them. The two past greats offer an insider perspective, talking about counting pitches, chin music, standing up the batter, and owning part of the plate, things only knowledgeable baseball fans appreciate with a sense for the history of the game.

Louis Clark "Lou" Brock played left field and batted left-handed, spending the rest of his career with the St. Louis Cardinals after a trade from the Chicago Cubs early in his career.

"Brock was born in El Dorado, Arkansas, and played college baseball at Southern University in Baton Rouge, Louisiana. He signed a contract with the Chicago Cubs as a free agent and broke into the major leagues in 1961. In his full rookie season of 1962, Brock became one of three players to hit a home run into the centerfield bleachers at the old Polo Grounds in New York. His blast came against Al Jackson in the second game of a doubleheader against the New York Mets and followed by

Hank Aaron's centerfield home run the next day. Joe Adcock was the first ballplayer to hit a ball over that wall, in 1953." [14]

The Cardinals' manager, Johnny Keanne, insisted on trying to attain Brock to increase team speed and help the batting order, struggling after the retirement of Stan Musial in 1963. The 1964 trade that brought Brock, Jack Spring. and Paul Toth to the Cardinals and Ernie Broglio, Bobby Shantz, and Doug Clemens to the Cubs, is one of the best trades in Cardinals history. At the time of the trade, the Cardinals had a record of twenty-eight wins and thirty-one losses and were in eighth place, trailing even the Cubs. Four months after the trade, the Cardinals won the World Series in seven games over the heavily favored New York Yankees.

Brock was the first player ever to bat in a major league game played in Canada, leading off the game against the expansion team Montreal Expos at Jerry Park in 1969.

Brock led the National League in stolen bases eight times and stole a major league record 118 stolen bases in 1974. Ricky Henderson later broke that record. Even though Henderson surpassed Brock's stolen base record, the National League honors the leader of stolen bases with the Lou Brock Award at the end of the regular season each year. Inducted into the Baseball Hall of Fame in 1985, the St. Louis Cardinals organization previously retired his number 20. Whenever he appears at games and steps onto the playing field, fans greet him with a loud cheer of "Lou, Lou, Lou," an appreciation for his gentlemanly ways and a gesture of a town's love for Lou Brock.

During his illustrious career, Brock won the 1967 Babe Ruth Award, the 1974 Major League Player of the Year Award, the prestigious 1975 Roberto Clemente Award, the 1977 Lou Gehrig Memorial Award, and the 1979 Hutch Award.

In 1974, Schnucks Grocers held a writing contest where kids wrote, in 250 words or less, why they wanted to become a batboy or batgirl for the St. Louis Cardinals. My sister Patricia was born on October 4, 1964, the day the Cardinals won the pennant before going on to beat the New York Yankees in the World Series that year. Entering the writing contest, Patricia explained that our parents threatened to name her "Cardinala" on the pennant-winning day she was born, eventually settling on the name Patricia. She went on to write that she was a ten-year-old pitcher on her softball team and a big fan of the Cardinals, Lou Brock being her favorite player.

She won the writing contest. At a Cardinals home game later that season, Lou Brock introduced himself to Dad, Mom, and sister Patricia, going out of his way to make them comfortable as he showed them around the dugout and clubhouse a couple of hours before the game. Patricia worked the game as an official Cardinals batgirl.

Hall of Fame shortstop Ozzie Smith took the meaning of playing defense to a higher level. Though he made hundreds of spectacular catches for many years as a shortstop for the St. Louis Cardinals in the eighties, probably his best defensive play occurred while he was playing shortstop for the San Diego Padres. Diving behind second base, the ball took a bad hop as Ozzie was nearly at a full stretch in midair. His glove hand pointing toward right field, he reached back and caught the ball with his bare hand as the front of his body slid in the dirt. With catlike agility, he bounced up seemingly all in one motion and threw out the runner at first base.

On opening day of each new season, fans looked forward to Smith's signature backflip while running out to his shortstop position at the start of the game. Smith won thirteen consecutive Gold Glove Awards and played in fifteen all-star games during his illustrious career.

In pursuit of Roger Maris's single season home run record, the 1998 home run chase between Mark McGwire and Sammy Sosa rekindled interest in baseball all across America. Every night, fans watched the late night sports news on television to see if either player hit a home run earlier in the day. Newspapers could not be printed fast enough, as people wanted to read everything about the chase. At season's end,

McGwire had seventy and Sosa had sixty-six home runs. Awards, celebrations, ceremonies, and all sorts of hoopla followed as baseball was back as one of the American staples: baseball, hot dogs, and apple pie. In St. Louis, a portion of Interstate 70 got a new name, designated the Mark McGwire Highway. Sammy Sosa appeared in numerous television commercials pushing products for Pepsi, Nike, McDonald's, and trying to sell video games.

After McGwire refused to comment on steroids use in his testimony before Congress in 2005, his legacy and his career statistics called into question any chance of his entry into the Hall of Fame in the future.

"Asking me or any other player to answer questions about who took steroids in front of television cameras will not solve the problem. If a player answers 'No,' simply, he will not be believed; if he answers 'Yes,' then he risks public scorn and endless government investigations. My lawyers have advised me that I cannot answer these questions without jeopardizing my friends, my family, and myself. I will say, however, that it remains a fact in this country that a man, any man is innocent unless proven guilty. I'm here to be positive about the subject." [15]

Mark McGwire

McGwire's friend Jose Canseco allegedly injected him with anabolic steroids. His bodybuilder brother, Jay McGwire, alleges that Mark used deca durabolin and that he introduced the performance-enhancing drugs to him in 1994. Durabolin helped McGwire with joint problems and recovery from back injuries, while human growth hormone helped increase his strength, making him leaner in the process. Brother Jay claims by his own admission that he was the first person to inject him with performance enhancing drugs. In 1998, a reporter caught McGwire with androstenedione in his locker at Busch Stadium. Apparently, andro, sometimes used to curb side effects of steroids, can cause damage to the liver, heart, kidneys and testicles.

To date, there has been no legal action ever taken against McGwire. However, his steroids testimony cost him public affection. Once thought of as a sure Hall of Famer, he received less than one-fourth of the necessary votes from sportswriters in his first year of eligibility.

John Francis "Jack" Buck was an American sportscaster to baseball fans, what Johnny Carson was to late night television and Walter Cronkite was to the national news. Best known for his work announcing Major League Baseball and St. Louis Cardinals games, he received the Ford C. Frick Award from the Baseball Hall of Fame and learned of his induction into the National Radio Hall of Fame in 1995.

Sitting on a lawn chair in the backyard listening to Jack broadcast a Cardinals game on the radio was almost as good as being at the game. He did not overanalyze the players; he told well-thought-out, interesting stories, and he treated other people with respect, yet the listener always knew exactly what was going on with the game on the field. His signature call, "That's a winner," punctuated Cardinals victories as soon as the game ended and the last batter declared out by the umpire.

One of Jack Buck's final public appearances was on September 17, 2001, at Busch Memorial Stadium in St. Louis.

It was the first night that the major leaguers resumed playing baseball since the terrorists attacked the twin towers in New York City on September 11, 2001. Although Buck was very sick, struggling from lung cancer, diabetes, a pacemaker, cataracts, sciatica, vertigo, and Parkinson's disease, he maintained his composure long enough to read a self-written patriotic poem during the pregame ceremonies. Buck once joked, "I wish I would get Alzheimer's, and then I could forget I have all this other stuff." The poem, titled "For America," described the feelings of our citizens. Here is the poem:

> *Since this nation was founded under God, more than 200 years ago,*
> *We have been the bastion of Freedom . . .*
> *The light is which keeps the free world Aglow.*
> *We do not covet the possessions of others; blessed with the bounties we share.*

*We have rushed to help other nations . . . anything . . .
anytime . . . anywhere . . .*
*War is just not our nature . . . we will not start it, but we will
end the fight.*
If we are involved, we shall be resolved to protect what we know is right.
*A cowardly foe has challenged us, one which strikes and then
hides from our view.*
*With one voice, we say there is no choice today; there is only one
thing to do.*
*Everyone is saying the same thing and praying that we end these
senseless moments we are living.*
As our fathers did before, we shall win this unwanted war.
So our children will enjoy the future, we will be giving. [16]

Jack Buck

Sportsman's Park was built in 1920 and was home of the St. Louis Cardinals baseball team until 1966. The organization built Busch Memorial Stadium at Stadium Plaza, which opened in 1966 and was home of the baseball team for forty years until it made more sense to construct another new stadium instead of fixing structural concerns and adding corporate box suites to the existing stadium. Therefore, on April 10, 2006, the St. Louis Cardinals opened their new retro-style downtown ballpark, complete with much wider concourses, more eateries, more restrooms, more concessions, and not a bad seat in the house.

Albert Pujols and the St. Louis Cardinals became the first team in almost one hundred years to win a World Series Championship in the inaugural season of a new ballpark. The new Busch Stadium also served as host for the 80th MLB All-Star Game, in July 2009, the fourth time St. Louis held the event. Baseball fans flocked to St. Louis for a weeklong celebration including a future stars game, a celebrity softball game, the home run derby, and the all-star game. With classic arched openings, creative use of old and new materials, from brick and concrete to exposed steel and paned glass panels, the ballpark is one of the most aesthetically pleasing stadium designs in the world. Also pleasing is watching the game's current best player, Cardinals first baseman, Albert Pujols.

An interesting play occurred in the baseball game at New Busch Stadium on the night of September 11, 2009. With Albert Pujols the base runner at second base and Matt Holiday the base runner at first base, Ryan Ludwick hit an almost sure double-play groundball directly toward the shortstop for the Atlanta Braves. As Pujols was running toward third base and in front of the shortstop, the ball hit him in the legs. The umpire ruled Pujols out and immediately called the play dead. He awarded Holiday second base and because of one of those strange procedures in the rulebook, Ludwick's stats were credited with a hit. Surely, Ludwick will take it, as the hit goes nicely with the 5-for-5 night earlier in the week when he had two home runs, two doubles off the outfield wall and a single. Ludwick holds the all-time major league single season record for home runs hit by a player who throws left-handed yet bats right-handed with 37, pretty good for a player who overcame surgeries to his leg, hip, and wrist.

Dad loved baseball and he had a keen sense for the history of the game. He passed down to me much of his knowledge of the game, especially noticing how many great Cardinal players had the first name George, his first name.

George Whiteman spent most of his career playing in the minor leagues and was the World Series hero in 1918, and never played again in the major leagues.

George Sisler was one of the greatest hitters in the game. In 1920, he had 257 hits and was a strong player in all aspects of the game. Sisler came close to becoming the first player to total twenty or more doubles, triples, and home runs all in the same season.

In 1921, George Toporcer became the first player in the majors, other than a pitcher, to play the game wearing glasses. A decent hitter whose glove-work left room for improvement, Toporser was a utility man; he hit .264 and had a pair of runs-batted-in in 53 at-bats in 1921. However, he did pave the way for other bespectacled players.

In 1922, Cardinals pitcher George Uhle became the first flamethrower since 1897 to reach twenty victories in a season.

George Watkins owns the record for the highest batting average by a rookie major leaguer, batting .373 in 1930. On October 2, 1930, Cardinals player Watkins became the first National League player to homer in his first World Series at bat. The Philadelphia Athletics beat the St. Louis Cardinals in six games, with pitcher George Earnshaw winning two games for the World Champions.

George McQuinn of the St. Louis Browns had a thirty-four-game hitting streak in 1938. On October 4, 1944, his opening-game homer gave the Browns their first-ever victory and only homer in a World Series game.

George Fallon was a Cardinals shortstop and the first batter to face fifteen-year-old Cincinatti Reds pitcher Joe Nuxhall when the youngster made his major league debut on June 10, 1944. Fallon played on the 1944 World Series Championship team.

The St. Louis Cardinals traded for National League all-star George Crow to play first base for retiring Stan Musial in 1963.

Cardinals player George "Silent George" Hendrick and his .302 batting average, 25 home runs, and 109 runs-batted-in, earned him a spot on the 1980 National League all-star team. Hendrick gained the nickname because he did not like talking to the press, fearful that they would twist his comments. [17]

George Herman Ruth, Jr.'s father owned and managed a tavern, working long days; he did not pay much attention to his son. The father signed over custody of his seven-year-old son to the Xaverian brothers, Catholic missionaries who ran St. Mary's Industrial School for Boys. During the boy's years at St. Mary's, his baseball skills were apparent at an early age. Surprisingly, he played catcher most often during those years on St. Mary's varsity baseball team.

Brother Mathias became a father figure and a disciplinarian to the boy. Brother Mathias would have a very positive influence on all aspects of the boy's life. The time spent with Brother Mathias not only helped hone the boy's baseball swing, but also the guidance and encouragement gave him much-needed support that would translate into the boy's unfettering love for underprivileged orphans in later years.

When George was nineteen years old, Jack Dunn, owner and manager of the Baltimore Orioles, recognized his talent and signed him to a contract. Already known as one of the best scouts in baseball, Dunn helped start George's career. When other players saw the strapping boy with the young-looking face, they referred to him as "Jack's newest babe". Ever since that connection, everyone called George Herman Ruth Jr. "the Babe."

In his first World Series game in 1916, Babe pitched fourteen innings, winning the game 2 to 1 in the longest complete game in the history of professional baseball. Though a great pitcher, he was even a greater hitter. After a brief stint with the Boston Red Sox, that organization traded Babe to the New York Yankees for a large sum of cash. In order to keep Babe's bat in the lineup, the Yankees delegated him to playing in the field, mostly right field and first base. He went on to hitting 714 home runs in his career, once hitting 60 home runs in one season.

Over the years, newspaper sports writers referred to Babe as "The Great Bambino," "The Sultan of Swat," and Yankee Stadium became known as "The House that Ruth Built." *The Associated Press* named George Herman "Babe" Ruth the greatest athlete of the century. Though he never played or coached for the St. Louis Cardinals, he is the monarch of baseball; the *Sporting News* named him the greatest baseball player of all time.

George Herman "Babe" Ruth was among the first five inductees into the Baseball Hall of Fame in 1936, along with Ty Cobb, Walter Johnson, Christy Mathewson, and Honus Wagner.

Dad's father left him at an early age, moving to Chicago and never returning to check on him. He never went to any of his son's little league baseball games, never watched him play all-star second base for the navy. The next time Dad would see his father was at his funeral. Though this weighed heavily on his shoulders during his life, my dad, George Walter Hubele, Jr., was Babe Ruth to me.

When playing for my high school baseball team, the Vianney Griffins, Dad shared a special moment with me. Summoned from the bench to pinch-hit, I had my first official at-bat on the high school varsity team. Our team did not have a hit in the game. Able to hit a line drive to right field on the second pitch, my single broke up a no-hitter. After the inning was over, the coach inserted me into the game as the catcher. It was the only game caught by me in three years playing on the baseball team. Though we lost the game, for a moment the hit made me feel like Babe Ruth, getting a hit in my first at-bat, getting to play catcher just the way Babe Ruth started, and a man named George (my dad) watching the game from the parking lot.

The new Busch Stadium, home of the Major League Baseball team, the St. Louis Cardinals, is located next to the Gateway Arch. The Gateway Arch, also known as the St. Louis Arch, rests at the top of the tiered steps rising from the downtown levee of the Mississippi River. From most open-air views inside the baseball stadium, the Gateway Arch overlooks and guards the centerfield bleacher seats in a majestic setting. The arch is a symbol of the start of Lewis and Clark's westward expansion and the pioneers who helped shape the American West. This incredible 630-foot-high stainless steel structure amazes hundreds of thousands of visitors each year.

A signature 230-foot-tall medieval-looking clock tower at Union Station, built in 1894, was St. Louis's most visible symbol before the construction of the Gateway Arch. During the Worlds Fair of 1904, the clock tower became the monument that helped put St. Louis on the map as an industrial powerhouse and a central crossroads for the railroads of the nation.

By reading the information about artifacts at the underground Westward Expansion Museum below the Gateway Arch or delving into some of the books offered at the gift shop, you find out things about Lewis and Clark. Lewis was a devoted writer and, during the expedition, wrote in his journal on a daily basis. According to documented testimony at the Westward Expansion Museum, Lewis had not written in his journals for weeks during an end leg of the return trip to St. Louis. Turns out during that time, one of Lewis's own soldiers "Peter Cruzatte," accidentally shot him in the buttocks. Cruzatte was a man known as an excellent fiddler but a terrible shooter, and was blind in one eye.

Lewis and Clark enlisted another man, John Coulter, to hunt food and fend off bears and mountain lions. His main weapon, a Hawkins steel pellet rifle, became the zenith of the mountain men in the Wild West. The rifle, popular during the early settlement years of St. Louis in the late 1700s, became the weapon of choice to kill buffalo. For a few years after the completion of the Lewis and Clark Expedition, John lived as a neighbor to Daniel Boone, but died of jaundice in 1813.

Another great museum, tucked away on a hill in a recessed section of land, is the Truman Presidential Library, on the other side of the state in Independence, Missouri. One of the smallest simplest exhibits makes one of the most powerful impressions. In a glass enclosure is a handwritten letter from the parents of a soldier killed in Korea. In the letter, they tell President Truman to keep their son's accompanying Purple Heart, because they say he was responsible for his death. Truman kept the letter and medal in the top drawer of his White House desk for the rest of his term in office to remind him of the huge responsibility entrusted to him by American citizens.

Sometimes a person wonders what it would be like to go back in time and live with the people two hundred or one hundred years ago. What would you tell Lewis and Clark or President Truman? If you are a baseball fan, you could start off by telling them about the St. Louis Cardinals. Moreover, if it were possible to stick around to see all the changes, it would be interesting to witness what baseball and our nation are like in another one hundred years.

"FAREWELL"

In May of 2004, when the doctors went in to check for reasons for Dad's headaches, they found six tumors that had spread to his brain. The doctors ruled out the possibilities of surgery, which is what you are supposed to do in situations of this nature, because there was no choice. Dad learned that biopsies turned up cancerous cells in a tumor in his esophagus--hardly good news, but a CT scan of his head showed six more tumors metastasized in his brain. Dad was given three to six months to live. All this cancer and so many modules, too numerous to count, had spread through his body. The prognosis was incurable cancer. When he and Mom stopped by my house to tell me all of this, Dad's voice was shaky. I could tell there was no real hope for us. I wanted to say something to reassure him, but all I could say is we will handle the experience as a family and I wished I could take some of the pain for him. In June, Dad decided to go through the agonizing chemotherapy and radiation treatments in hopes of buying a little more time.

On one famous episode of "Seinfeld," Jerry tells the story of the last big box. Most people spend their lifetime moving from house to house, moving belongings in boxes. So much time spent working to accumulate more and more things to put in boxes. Everyone's last big move uses a beautiful box with nice big, shiny handles. Trouble is you are in the box (your coffin). Dad bought his first house in 1952 and lived in that house until his death on September 25, 2004. Life was full of wonderful talks, experiences, and fun events, just not a lot of boxes.

The day after Dad passed away, I wrote his obituary. It is very difficult to condense the full circle of a great man's life into a story of just a few brief paragraphs. There are not enough pages in a book to write about Dad's love for his wife and his children.

Finnegans Wake, written by Irish author James Joyce over a period of seventeen years, is a funny fictitious novel about a man's dreams, relationships, and his sons' struggles to carry on his legacy after his death. James Joyce writes with a circular view of life. Though my father and I had a great relationship, our legacy will only reach *"almost full circle"* as the Hubele surname became extinct with the two of us. Grandpa is gone and he had no brothers. Dad is gone and he had no brothers, and his only son had no sons. There will be no more comparisons made about father and son that our eyes looked alike or our voices sounded the same on the telephone. No matter what takes place the rest of my life, without a son to carry on the surname, the circle will not be complete. It will have an opening, an opening for my two daughters, Amanda and Allison, to spread some of their grandpa's messages to their children with a different name.

George Walter Hubele, 74, of St. Louis, entered into eternal rest on Saturday, September 25, 2004. He was the beloved husband of Audrey Margaret Hubele (*nee* Juengst); dearest father of Steven of St. Louis, Kathy (Dave) Hale of Denver, Colorado, Karen (Michael) Meyer of Arnold, and Patricia (David) Hoffman of Chesterfield. He was the dear grandfather of Amanda, Lindsay, Allison, Sydney, Bradley, and Connor; brother of Rita (Richard) Haupt and Dorothy (Richard) Heinlein; brother-in-law of Rose Holley-Mock and Charles Harvey; our dear uncle, cousin and friend to many.

Mr. Hubele served in the United States Navy from 1948-1952, partially during the Korean War. He was a sales manager for Metropolitan Life Insurance Company for the next thirty-five years. During those same years, he also served as a past president of the Retirees Veterans Association. After retirement, Mr. Hubele enjoyed working part-time at Sunset Lakes Golf Course.

He was a past member of the Elks Affton Chapter, a founding member of St. Simon Parish and a fixture as a fan at Affton Athletic Association.

Funeral is from the Kutis Affton Chapel at 10151 Gravois Road on Wednesday, September 29, at 9:00 a.m. to St. Simon the Apostle Catholic Church for Mass. Interment follows at Jefferson Barracks National Cemetery. Thank you in advance for any memorials to the American Cancer Society or St. Anthony's Hospice program at 10016 Kennerly Road, 63128. Visitation is Tuesday, 3:00-9:00 p.m.

Four days after Dad's passing, I gave the eulogy at the Kutis Affton Chapel inside the funeral home, and this was an honor of the highest regard.

Dad was born Sept 14, 1930, and he died Sept 25, 2004. I would like to think of his time as a celebration where Dad "passed the way" not passed away. On the night that we found out that Dad had esophageal and brain cancer, I was working and driving around in my parking lot sweeper at Arnold Bowling Alley, many thoughts running through my mind. I was wishing that there could be a sign telling me that everything would be okay. It was hard to believe (I only told my Aunt Rose at the time), but when I looked up into the sky, there was but one cloud and it began to take on the startling likeness of Jesus's head and face, with long hair and beard.

On the night Dad died, I was sitting with Mom and brother-in-law Mike. As we often did, we were watching the Cardinals baseball game. As Albert Pujols was up to the plate, I boldly predicted he would hit a home run. The next pitch, Pujols connected. The next day the headlines in the paper read, "Pujols Joins Company of Joe DiMaggio and Ted Williams." Well Dad joined the company of his dad and God.

During his battle, Dad never once complained and he never lost his sense of humor; he joked with everyone right to the end. He inspired us all at work and play. Kathy flew in three times from Denver, sleeping at the hospital and assisting with medical advice. Karen cooked for all of us, cleaned, and found supplies to keep Dad comfortable. Patti assisted with nutritional matters and phone calls. We had some wonderful doctors and nurses, who tried their best. We want to thank all our family and friends, who called, visited, sent cards and letters, or brought food. Special thanks go to the superhuman beings of the hospice program.

Those of us who loved Dad and took him to his rest today pray that what he was to us and what he wished for others will someday come to pass for all the world. Mom and Dad, you both deserve the biggest matching gold medals that can be made. Lastly, we love you, Mom, and will miss you, Dad, because together you were the best and your children were incredibly lucky to have you both as our parents.

The patriarch of our family, Dad waged a valiant struggle with many chemotherapy and radiations treatments, succumbing to a summer long battle with brain cancer. On September 29, 2004, laid to rest at Jefferson Barracks National Cemetery, Dad joins other distinguished persons and deceased service members who protected our great country from past dictators and terrorists. At the burial ceremony, Dad received full military honors on behalf of a grateful nation, a full-gun salute, a United States flag, and navy dog tags dated May 12, 1948, presented to Mom. In turn, Mom presented the flag and dog tags to me, both items cherished as my most prized possessions for the rest of my life.

Here are some words from a great leader, Shawnee Indian Chief Tecumseh, and his writings entitled, *Looking for Some Peace*. "When your time comes to die, be not like those whose hearts are filled with the fear of death, so that when their time comes, they weep and pray for a little more time to live their lives over again in a different way. Instead, sing your death song, and die like a hero going home."

Nearly five years after Dad died, upon returning home from visiting my dad's grave on September 11, 2009, the eighth anniversary of the terrorist attacks on the World Trade Center and the Pentagon, a national newscaster reported a story on the television evening news about the world's oldest known person. "Gertrude Baines, who once quipped she had won the genetic lottery, born in Shellman, Georgia in 1894, died today; she died at the age of 115 years old. At the time of her birth, Grover Cleveland was president, the only president to serve two non-consecutive terms in office. An African-American woman and the grandmother of slaves, Gertrude lived long enough to vote for Barack Obama for president," reported the newscaster.

Following are some of the distinguished persons buried at Jefferson Barracks National Cemetery.

Eliza Ann Lash was the first person buried at Jefferson Barracks National Cemetery on August 5, 1827. She was an infant of an officer stationed at Jefferson Barracks Army Depot.

The 56th United States Colored Troops Monument pays tribute to the 56th Infantry Regiment of the United States Colored Troops. The obelisk dedication honors the memory of the 175 soldiers of the 56th USCT who died of cholera in August of 1866.

There are 1,104 Confederate dead buried at Jefferson Barracks National Cemetery, 824 soldiers, 161 civilians, 2 civilian women, 1 gunboat crewman, 1 identified only as a "conscript," 100 not identified as soldier or civilian, and 15 confederates are unknown.

George Hobday, awarded the medal of bravery in action for his service at Wounded Knee Creek, South Dakota, fought during the Indian

War of 1890. After reenlisting at the St. Louis Military Depot, he died of pneumonia two months later. Buried under the misspelled name of "George Holday," but now corrected, and he has a new Medal of Honor headstone.

Hugh Stanley Miller served as a sergeant in the United States Marine Corps. He became a Major League Baseball player, a first baseman who played just one game for the Philadelphia Phillies in 1911.

William John Miller, a St. Louis native, served in World War I. After the war, he played in Major League Baseball for the St. Louis Browns in 1920 and 1921; he also played for manager Ty Cobb and the Detroit Tigers in 1925.

Henry Townsend, rhythm and blues guitarist and songwriter, wrote and published hundreds of songs. In the 1930s, he played with blues greats Roosevelt Sykes, Walter Davis, and Robert Johnson. While serving in the Army during World War II and way ahead of his time, many feel a commanding officer wrongfully discharged him for protesting civil rights issues.

Bruce Avery Van Voorhis served his country as a lieutenant commander in the United States Navy. He "displayed gallantry and intrepidity at the risk of his life above and beyond the call of duty" as he executed six missions to demolish the enemy's vital radio command station on Japanese held Greenwich Island during the Battle of the Solomon Islands, July 6, 1943.

St. Louis native Bill Keenoy, George Patton's Driver during World War II, rests in peace at Jefferson Barracks National Cemetery.

Michael Joseph Blassie, a graduate of the United States Air Force Academy, was shot down and killed in South Vietnam. His remains, buried in Arlington National Cemetery's Tomb of the Unknowns, were later identified as a soldier from the Vietnam War. After petitioning the United States government for permission, the family was allowed to bring his body home to rest at Jefferson Barracks National Cemetery.

Hall of Fame sportscaster John "Jack" Buck served with the United States Army during World War II. In 1943, Buck became a corporal and instructor with K Company, 47th Regiment, and 9th Infantry Division. On March 15, 1945, while crossing the Remagen Bridge into Germany to try to help stop enemy fire, shrapnel wounded Buck in his left leg and forearm. After spending time in a Paris hospital, he received a Purple Heart. After the war, he enrolled at Ohio State University, beginning his career at the campus radio station. In 1954, he announced the St. Louis Cardinals baseball games collaborated with Harry Carry for many years. In addition to Cardinals games, he also announced Super Bowl games, World Series games, and nationally televised professional bowling events. He belongs to the Baseball Hall of Fame, Broadcaster's Hall of Fame, and the Radio Hall of Fame.

Elizabeth Seifert, buried at Jefferson Barracks National Cemetery, wrote fifty-one books and her last novel, *Two Doctors, Two Lies* was published in 1982.

Oliver Sain was musician, saxophone player, songwriter, and producer of work recorded by such artists as the Allman Brothers Band, Chaka Khan, and Loretta Lynn. His best-known songs are "Bus Stop" and "Feel Like Dancing."

First Lieutenant Daniel P. Riordan, graduate of Vianney High School and Southeast Missouri State University, a heroic St. Louis native, served his country as first lieutenant of First Cavalry Division of the United States Army stationed out of Fort Hood, Texas. Killed in Iraq by a roadside bomb during a mission northwest of Baghdad, he received the Combat Infantryman's Badge, the Purple Heart, and the Bronze Star, and rests in peace at Jefferson Memorial Cemetery.

Each year, on the Sunday prior to Memorial Day, former Missouri State Representative Anthony Dill and hundreds of boy scouts and cub scouts spend countless hours placing flags on the graves of more than 175,000 soldiers. Year after year, hundreds of people go to Veteran's Day parades, while hundreds of thousands go to St. Patrick's Day parades where half the drunks in the world go to party. Despite the disproportionate level of patriotism, Dill and his volunteers have never waived on their work. Representative Dill has distributed flags on the graves for sixty consecutive years. "It's just a special recognition for those who died in action and those who have died afterward," Dill says. [18]

It is mind-boggling to think about how fighting wars has changed in the past two hundred years. The military now buys more unmanned drones than they buy fighter jets. Pilots manage land-based cockpits built inside trailers to control the drones flying 7,500 miles away in Afghanistan. Eyes in the sky provide much needed air support for ground forces in Iraq and Afghanistan. Cameras mounted in the front of the drones and operated by remote control see everything on the ground from two miles away high up in the sky. Soldiers fight wars much differently today, but thousands of ground forces still do the dangerous work fighting terrorists in traditional ways of combat.

Americans enjoy freedom on a day-to-day basis and soldiers we have never met fight for it. As a reminder, remember to thank our war veterans and the young men and women fighting for our freedom in Iraq and Afghanistan.

FOOTNOTES AND ILLUSTRATION CREDITS

1. *http://en.Wikipedia.org/wiki/woodstock_festival*, the free encyclopedia, this article is about Woodstock festival.
2. *St. Louis Post-Dispatch, South County Suburban Newspaper*, by John Stoeffler, July 2008, article about abortion.
3. Testimony before the Constitution Subcommittee of the House Judiciary Committee, by Gianna Jessen, April 22, 1996.
4. Oklahoma State University Library, *The Kappler Project: Indian Affairs, Laws and Treaties; Treaty with the Shawnee 1825* (Articles 4 and 5)
5. *Kids Today Magazine*, St. Louis Children's Hospital, Fall 2009 Issue, page 3, article by Leonard Bacharier, MD, clinical director of pediatric allergy, immunology and pulmonary medicine.
6. *Cross Country, by Robert Sullivan*, Chapter 3, and second paragraph of article on page 99.
7. *http://en.Wikipedia.org/wiki/Pearl_Harbor*, the free encyclopedia, article chronicles attack of Pearl Harbor, first paragraph, page 5 of 7.

8. *http://en.Wikipedia.org/wiki/Pearl_Harbor*, the free encyclopedia, article chronicles attack of Pearl Harbor, pages 7 and 8 of 19.
9. United States Department of Education's National Commission, published a report, "Excellence and Education, a Nation at Risk," 1983.
10. *Suburban Journals Newspaper, Parade Magazine*, October 11, 2009 issue, article entitled "Be Part of the Solution" by Matt Damon, pp. 4-5.
11. *www.rogershornsby.com* Web site is devoted to life of professional baseball player Rogers Hornsby.
12. *Baseball as I Have Known It*, written by Fred Lieb, Temp Publishing, 1970.
13. *The Rock Community Newspaper*, July 2009 Issue, "History of St. Louis Cardinals All-Star Games," pp 17-18, there is no mention of author of article.
14. *http://en.wikipedia.org/wiki/Lou_Brock*, pp 1-2, this is a free encyclopedia Web site.
15. Testimony before Congress in 2005, comments on steroid use, broadcast on national television. These are McGwire's own words.
16. *Jack Buck, a Collection of Poems and Stories*, published for Gateway Cystic Fibrosis Foundation, written by Jack Buck to benefit Cystic Fibrosis, eighteen poems in book.
17. *The Baseball Chronicle, History of Major League Baseball*, published in 2004 by Publications International, Ltd., written by David Nemec, Stephen Hanks, Dick Johnson, David Raskin, Thomas W. Gilbert, Andy Cohen, Joe Glickman, Danny Green, Stuart Shea.
18. Jefferson Barracks Cemetery Web site, records 1 through 51, *www.findagrave.com/php/famous.php*

INDEX

A

abortion, 37-43, 164
Alaska, 133-34, 138, 142-43
Alaskans, 136, 141, 144
Amanda, definition of, 45
American Bandstand, 32
American Kennel Club, 20
"America Today" (Allison Hubele), 68
Angelina (cashier from the Philippines), 131-32
Annie (from Kentucky Beach and Spa Resort), 85
Armstrong, Neil, 104
Association of Reproductive Health Professionals, 42
Averill, Earl, 172

B

Babe Ruth, 178, 185-87
Baines, Gertrude, 193
Baker's Field, 25, 35-36
Banks, Ernie, 175
Barack, 193
Battleship Missouri Memorial, 149
beagle, 20, 56, 96
Becker (friend of Steven Hubele), 26, 34
beekeepers, 101
Big D (friend of Steven Hubele), 25-26, 32, 36
Bigley, Mark, 26, 74, 76, 78
Bigley, Morgan, 76
Bitsy (dog), 20
Blackie (Kathy's fish), 22

Black Mountain Glacier, 138
Blassie, Michael Joseph, 194-95
Bob (employee at *St. Louis Post-Dispatch*), 31
Boeing 707, 20
Boone, Daniel, 188
Breakfast Mac, 123
British Open, 75, 86
Brock, Louis Clark, 177-79
Broglio, Ernie, 178
Brooklyn Dodgers, 173
Bruce, Steve, 107
Buck, Jack. *See* Buck, John Francis
Buck, John Francis, 29, 66, 176, 181, 195
   "For America," 181
Buffet, Warren
   Snowball, 159
Burkett, Jesse, 170
Busch Stadium, 173, 175, 180, 183, 187
Bush, George W., 156, 167

C

Canseco, Jose, 180
Car, Greg, 103
Carey, Harry, 29, 66
Carson, Johnny, 181
Casa Botin, 121-22
Center of Disease Control and Prevention, 105, 162
Charlotte's Web (White), 10
Chicago Cubs, 95, 172, 175, 177
Chinatown, 145
Chugach Mountains, 136, 139
Clark, William, 75
Clemens, Doug, 178
Clemente, Roberto, 175, 178
Cobb, Ty, 171, 174, 186, 194
colony collapse disorder, 101
Costner, Kevin, 53-54
Cotton Planter, 22
Coulter, John, 187
Creedence Clearwater Revival, 33
Crenshaw, Willis, 21
Cronkite, Walter, 181
Crow, George, 185
Cruzatte, Peter, 187
curriculum, 154, 156, 158
Cynthia (friend of Allison Hubele), 50-52

D

Darwin, Bernard, 78
Darwin, Charles, 78
Dean, Jay Hanna. *See* Dizzy Dean
Dean, Paul, 172
Debbie Hilarious, 25-26
DeFoe, William, 176
DeGrand, Thomas D., 81
Derski, Spider, 78
devil's playground, 60

Dewey, John, 156
Diamond Head Crater, 150
Dierbergs, 131
Dierker (parish priest), 27
Dill, Anthony, 196
Dizzy Dean, 171-72
Dole Plantation, 150
Donnybrook, 108
Dorsey, Jack, 160
DOT (Department of Transportation), 108
Dressel Public School, 25
Drysdale, Don, 175
Duke, Michael, 110
Dunn, Jack, 185
Dylan, Bob, 34

E

Earnshaw, George, 184
Easy Cheese, 130
Easy Rider, 34
education, 41, 59-60, 135, 151-55, 157-59, 164-65. *See also* parents; teachers
Einstein, Albert, 153
elephants, 103
Elliot's, 28
Emerson, Ralph Waldo, 44
Environmental Protection Agency, 169
Eskimos, 134-35

F

Fairmont Park, 22
Fallon, George, 184-85
fatherhood, 5, 41, 43-45, 53, 71
Faust, Drew Gilpin, 163
Field of Dreams, 53
Finnegans Wake (Joyce), 190
Fogerty, John, 33
"For America" (Buck), 181
Forest Park, 78, 80
Francis, Connie, 33
Franklin, Benjamin, 87
"Free Bird" (Lynyrd Skynyrd), 36
Fuchida, Mitsuo, 149

G

Gateway Arch, 187
Gateway Hotel, 31
Genda, Minoru, 149
generation gap, 33, 63, 65
Gibson, Bob
  Sixty Feet, Six Inches, 30, 175-77
Goldie (Steven Hubele's fish), 22
golf, 5, 58, 65-66, 71-82, 85-86, 166, 171, 191
Gore, Al, 167-68
Granada Show, 26
Grandpa's Horse, 23-24
Gravois Auto Repair, 62-63
Gravois Creek, 22, 25, 50

Great Flood of 1993, 166
grocery chains, 131, 178
Gunner. *See* Trammel, Train
Gutenberg, Johannes, 9

H

Hacker, Joe, 81
Hackman, Gene, 176
Hagen (brigadier general), 147
   War in the Pacific, 147
Hagen, Jerome T., 147
Harris, Richard, 135
Harry Potter, 9-10
Hawaii, 5, 17, 34, 119, 133, 146-47, 150
Heimburger's Bakery, 25, 35
Hemingway, Ernest, 122
Henderson, Ricky, 178
Hendrick, George, 185
Hilton, Conrad, 31
Hilton Hawaiian Village Beach Resort, 145
Historical Research Center, 22
Hitler, Adolf, 38
Hobday, George, 193-94
Hogan, Ben, 78, 80
Hogan, Homer, 78, 80
Holday, George. *See* Hobday, George
Holdover, Gene, 74
Home Depot, 127

honeybees, 101-2, 104, 106
Hoosie (friend of Steven Hubele), 26, 32
Hornsby, Rogers, 171
Howard, Ron, 10
Hubele, Allison Nicole
   "America Today," 68
   birthday, 57
   definition of name, 45
   first assignment at school, 53
   graduation from Mehlville High School, 70
   as a grown-up, 68
   letter to Tooth Fairy, 53
   receiving her driver's license, 62
Hubele, Amanda Marie, 7, 44-48, 107, 124-25, 148, 190
Hubele, Audrey Margaret (née Juengst), 7-8, 13, 17-18, 152, 190
Hubele, Carl, 22
Hubele, George (grandfather), 22
Hubele, George Walter, Jr.
   buying a beagle, 20
   death, 66, 190
   first meeting with Audrey, 17
   as a married man, 17
   scoring hole-in-one, 76
   at seventeen, 17
Hubele, Steven Michael
   birth, 20
   at a Cardinals game, 30
   childhood, 21, 25-26, 32, 35-36, 123

defining moment, 38-40
encounter with an old man in a wheelchair, 132
encounter with Debbie Hilarious, 25, 35, 51, 73
eulogy, 191-92
experience at the church, 27
falling from a manhole, 109
first experience at a horse racetrack, 22-24
first Father's Day without a father, 65
as a golfer, 73
household, 18-19
job at Concord Bowling Lanes and Swimming Pool, 28
letter about the nation's school systems, 59
locked from his house, 56, 58
moments with Allison, 50-52, 54
moments with Amanda, 45, 47
as a paper boy, 86, 88-89, 98, 100
playing Scrabble, 128
as a proud father, 44-45, 133
stung by bees, 104-5
trip to Anchorage with Allison, 133, 143
trip to Kentucky Lake, 83
trip to Oahu, 150
visit to Pearl Harbor, 150
Hunt, Ron, 176

I

Iditarod Trail Race, 140-42
Imperial Japanese Navy, 148
Internet, 59, 107, 142, 156, 161. *See also* safety; Web sites

J

Jackson, Al, 177
Jackson, Joe, 54
Jackson, Reggie
  Sixty Feet, Six Inches, 177
James, Tommy, 34
Johnson, Walter, 186
Jones, James Earl, 54
Joyce, James
  Finnegans Wake, 190
Juneau, Joe, 135

K

Karen (sister of Steven Hubele), 18, 27, 57, 190, 192
Kathy (sister of Steven Hubele), 18, 21-22, 27, 109, 190, 192
Keanne, Johnny, 178
Keenoy, Bill, 194
Kennedy, John F., 21, 33
Kennedy, Robert, 21
Kentucky Lake, 83
Kerr, Dickie, 173

Kimberly (wife of Steven Hubele), 124-26
King, Martin Luther, 21
Kinsella, Ray, 54
Kirkwood, 38
kitty wicks, 139
Kohler (owner of Kohler's farm), 35
Koufax, Sandy, 30, 175
Ku Klux Klan, 176
kulolo, 151

L

Laclede Groves, 88
Lamb of Arms, 22
Lancaster, Burt, 54
Lash, Eliza Ann, 192-93
Lauer, Matt, 127, 129
lawnmower, 107, 127-28, 169
Led Zeppelin, 33, 36
   "Stairway to Heaven," 36
Lee, Aura, 140
letters
   Anonymous, 96
   Apartment #1535, 95
   Betty S., 98-99
   Daeger, 93
   Harold R., 97
   John B., 97
   King Bossett, 91
   Mr. and Mrs. Mitchum and Dog Peaches, 96
   Mr. Pratton, 95
   Mrs. C. W., 93
   Mrs. G. Fanthouse, 90
   Mrs. Miller, 92
   Ralph C., 99
   Vern, 93
Lewis and Clark Expedition, 187-88
Lieb, Fred, 171
Lifeport Transporters, 111
Liotta, Ray, 54
Looking for Some Peace (Tecumseh), 192-93
lots of curb appeal, 55, 102, 106-8, 110
Lou (owner of Lou's Sinclair Gas Station), 35, 66
Lowrey, Janette Sebring
   The Poky Little Puppy, 10
Ludwick, Ryan, 183
Lynyrd Skynyrd
   "Free Bird," 36

M

Mac (baseball coach), 31
Mackey, Dick, 142
Madigan, Amy, 54
Mahimahi, 151
mahouts, 103
Major League Baseball, 31, 170-72, 176, 181, 187, 194

"The Man, the Truck, the Moment: Parking Lot Business Is Taking Off," 106
Mann, Terence, 54
Maris, Roger, 179
Mathewson, Christy, 186
Mathias (father figure to Babe Ruth), 185
McCarver, Tim, 80, 174
McDonald's, 97, 123-24, 160, 180
McGwire, Jay, 180
McGwire, Mark, 179-80
McQuinn, George, 184
Meramec River, 75, 167
Meyer, Mike, 83
Miller, Hugh Stanley, 194
Miller, Johnny, 78
Miller, Mitch, 33
Miller, William John, 194
Missouri American Water Company, 168
Missouri Partnership for Parenting Assistance and Literacy Investment for Tomorrow, 157
Mitchell, Joni, 34
Mize, Larry, 78
Morris, Tom, 75
motivation, 153
Musial, Stan, 170, 172-74, 178, 185

N

Nagumo (Japanese leader), 149
National Right to Life and Human Life International, 42
neighborhood, 14, 17, 19, 25, 34-36, 38, 46, 50-51, 56, 61, 87, 108, 159
New York Giants, 173
New York Yankees, 30, 178-79, 186
Norman, Greg, 78
Nuxhall, Joe, 173, 185

O

Oahu, 119, 145-46, 150
Oak Hill Country Club, 75
Obama, Barack, 193
Obama, Michelle, 162
Ohshit, Dick, 74
One-Eyed Monster, The, 26
Operation Clean Stream, 167

P

Page, Jimmy, 36
parents, 45, 49, 59-61, 70, 155-57, 162, 164-65, 192
Pate, Jerry, 75
Patricia (sister of Steven Hubele), 18, 178-79, 190
Pearl Harbor, 17, 145-46, 148-50

Peggy (neighbor friend of Kimberly Hubele), 125
Perry Rhodan, 9
Pieper (neighbor of Steven Hubele), 29
Pitt, Brad, 10-11
Plant, Robert, 36
Poky Little Puppy, The (Lowrey), 10
pollination, 101. *See also* honeybees
pollution, 168-69
Polynesian Cultural Center, 151
Preis, Afred, 146
Presley, Elvis, 33
Price, Nick, 75
Pro-Am Golf Center, 81-82
Professional Golfers Association of America, 81
Prudhoe Bay, 136
public schools, 157, 159
Pujols, Albert, 183, 191-92

R

Redington, Joe, Jr., 141
Redington, Joe, Sr., 141
Reuter (doctor), 17
Richey, Branch, 173
Riddles, Libby, 142
Riordan, Daniel P., 196
River des Peres, 167
Roe v. Wade, 42
Roland, Johnny, 21

Ronnie's Drive-In, 25, 34-35
Roosevelt, Franklin D., 145, 149
Ruth, George Herman, Jr. *See* Babe Ruth

S

safety, 55, 83, 155-56, 161. *See also* school lunch programs
Sain, Oliver, 195
salmon, 139-40
  lomi, 151
Sam (from Kentucky Beach and Spa Resort), 85
Santa Claus, 50-52
Sarazen, Gene, 78
Schnucks, 131, 178
school lunch programs, 162
Seifert, Elizabeth, 195
semelparity, 140
Shantz, Bobby, 178
Shawnee Indians, 75
Shitsie (name of the beagle), 20
Shop 'n Save, 131
Simper, Skippy, 29-31
Simpers family, 29
Sinatra, Frank, 33
Sisler, George, 184
Sixty Feet, Six Inches (Jackson and Gibson), 177
Skinker Avenue, 79-80
Smith, Ozzie, 179

Snowball (Buffet), 159
Sosa, Sammy, 179-80
Sourdough, Dusty, 140
Sourdough Mining Company Restaurant, 140
South Lindbergh Boulevard, 25, 47
Spring, Jack, 178
"Stairway to Heaven" (Led Zeppelin), 36
Star Wars, 9-10
Statler Hotel, 28, 31
Stengel, Casey, 175
Steve Hubele Incorporated, 88, 106
St. Louis Cardinals, 21, 29-31, 66, 121, 169-79, 181, 183-88, 191, 195
St. Louis Post-Dispatch, 31, 42, 76, 87, 89-90, 93, 96, 106-7
Stoeffler, John, 42
St. Simons Church, 25, 27
Suburban Journals, 87
Sullivan, Robert, 123
Sunnen Lake, 57
Sunset Lakes, 73, 75-76, 166, 191
Swenson, Rick, 142

T

Tad (friend of Steven Hubele), 26
Taylor, James, 33
teachers, 43, 53, 59-60, 68, 107, 152-58, 160-63, 165
  problems, 164
Teach for America, 158
Tecumseh (Shawnee Indian chief), 192
Thunderbird, 20
TIF (tax-increment financing), 159
Toad (Steven Hubele's friend), 26, 36
Toporcer, George, 184
Toth, Paul, 178
Townsend, Henry, 194
Trammel, Train, 72-73
Treaty of St. Louis, 75
Truman, Harry, 188
Tull, Jethro, 34

U

Uhle, George, 184
United States Department of Education's National Commission, 164
USS *Arizona* Memorial, 119-20, 145-46
USS *Missouri*, 150
USS *Ward*, 149

V

Van Voorhis, Bruce Avery, 194
Veldon, John, 28
vertigo, 105, 181

vestibular system, 105
Vianney Griffins, 186
Vietnam War, 20, 33, 147, 195

W

Wagner, Honus, 186
Waikiki, 145, 150-51
Walmart, 110, 127
War in the Pacific (Hagen), 147
Washburn, Ray, 175
Watkins, George, 184
Watson, Tom, 86
Weaver, Doug, 75
Web sites, 59, 155, 160-61
White, Bill, 30-31
White, E. B.
   Charlotte's Web, 10
Whiteman, George, 184
Whittier, 116, 138
Wiebe, Mark, 75

Wildcat, Tom, 74, 76
Wilder, Tom, 76
William (baseball coach), 31
Wills, Maury, 174
Woods, Tiger, 75, 86
Woodstock, 33-34
World Series, 30, 172, 175, 177-79, 183-86, 195
World War II, 20, 93, 146-49, 173, 194-95
Worths, Jim, 83

Y

Yamamoto, Isoroku, 148
YMCA Lodge, 57-58

Z

Zimmern, Andrew, 102-3

Get Published, Inc!
Thorofare, NJ 08086
16 February, 2010
BA2010047